The Man
Who Wrestled
With God

*Light from the Old Testament
on the
Psychology of Individuation*

John A. Sanford

PAULIST PRESS
New York/Ramsey

Acknowledgments:
To Helen Macey for her invaluable help in
editing the manuscript,
To Ruth Budd for her help in preparing the
material for publication, and
To the members of my Bible Study Group at
St. Paul's Episcopal Church, San Diego,
who helped me understand the stories.
Unless indicated otherwise, all Biblical
quotations are from The Jerusalem Bible.

Library of Congress
Catalog Card Number: 80-84829

ISBN: 0-8091-2367-3

Published by Paulist Press
545 Island Road, Ramsey, N.J. 07446

Printed and bound in the
United States of America

CONTENTS

dedicated to
my daughter Katie

INTRODUCTION

What's In A Story?

Laurens van der Post, the South African explorer and author who once lived for many months with the Bushmen of the Kalahari Desert, had as one of his main objectives the collecting of the stories, the folktales, of these very primitive people. But though he persisted for many months, every inquiry he directed to them was met by blank looks, or a denial that any such stories existed. Only after he had known the shy little people for a long time, and they had accepted him as a trusted friend, did they finally share with him their fascinating tales about the origin of the world, the first man, how the animals were created, and the other narratives which made up the collective folk-treasure of this remote and little known people. Van der Post realized that the Bushmen had hesitated for so long to share their stories with him because they believed the stories somehow contained their very soul as a people; and that if any enemy should come into possession of the stories he would have the means to destroy them spiritually.

This is how important stories are to a primitive people like the Kalahari Bushmen. But any child could have told us the same thing. For in an almost exactly similar way archetypal (folk or fairy) stories relate a child to *his* soul; they are healing to his spirit, enriching to his imagination. I recall a time when

a couple visiting us in Southern California took their small
son on an excursion to nearby Tijuana, Mexico. It was a frightfully hot day, the traffic was terrible, the border town was
jammed, and there was a long wait in the car before the family
could get back into the United States. By the time they reached
San Diego the little boy was completely fragmented, a burden
to himself and an irritation to everyone around him. Something
said to me, "He needs a story." So I told him the fairy tale
of Hansel and Gretel, and the terrible witch who almost did
them in, but who was tricked in the nick of time by the clever
and resourceful children. The little fellow listened wide-eyed
and silent. When I finished, he climbed down from his chair
without a word, and quietly went out to play. He had simply
lost touch with his soul on that tedious and ghastly automobile
journey; the story brought him back together again.

But stories are for everyone, not just for primitive people
and children. A friend of mine, the Rev. Allen Whitman (author
of "Pray For Your Life", Augsburg Publishing House) talks
about what he calls the "theology of story."[1] Fr. Whitman
points out that the Bible is one vast story of God's action
in history, and of His interaction with a series of men and
women. Christianity is also story; if you listen to the words
of the Creed you will hear, not a statement of doctrine, but
a summation of the adventure story of Christ, the God-man.
The Eucharist is story too: in fact, the priest at the altar re-
enacts the happenings at the Last Supper, the Crucifixion, and
the Resurrection. When you get right down to it, our whole
lives, and even our dreams, are stories. I remember the first
dream my small daughter excitedly reported. She came to the
breakfast table and declared, "Last night I had a bear story:
and *I* was *in* it." The power of Christianity does not lie in
the overlayers of theological doctrine, but in the power of the
Christian story to affect us.

Jesus, too, knew the power of story; the great bulk of
his teachings are in a special story form which we call the

---

[1] Allen Whitman, *A Gospel Comes Alive,* Meditations on St. John's Gospel
Informed by a Theology of Story and Play, St. Paul, Minnesota: Macalester
Park Publishing Co., 1974.

parable. Through his parables Jesus is able to reach us on a level deeper than the intellectual, and to lead us to insights which a didactic or conceptualized form of teaching could never impart.

One reason for the power of story as a teaching medium is that it gets our attention. No learning can take place until this happens. A farmer once offered to sell a mule to a friend, assuring him that this mule was most cooperative and would do anything he asked. The friend was delighted and bought the mule, but next day when he told the mule to pull his cart the mule simply stood still. He ordered the mule to pull his plow, but the mule didn't budge. Exasperated, he called the farmer to complain, and the farmer came right over. Taking a length of 2 x 4 he swung with all his force and hit the mule a terrible blow on the rump. "Now," he cried, "pull that plow!" And the mule pulled. "I thought you told me this mule was so cooperative he would do anything I asked," the friend said, bewildered. "He will," the farmer replied, "only first you have to get his attention."

That's the way it is with us. God has to get our attention. Many times He can do this only by dealing us some mighty blow. But we are better off if He can reach us with a story, which is a great attention-getter, and a powerful means of communicating as well.

The stories selected for retelling in this book are the tales of Jacob, Joseph, Moses, and Adam and Eve. All these stories are extremely ancient. Biblical scholars tell us that they come from the oldest traditions which make up the Old Testament. No doubt they were circulated by word-of-mouth for many centuries before they were committed to writing. The stories raise all kinds of questions for scholars, and, of course, challenge our credulity. Some scholars, for instance, doubt their authenticity. Jacob, some say, never really lived; the story was invented to explain the origins of the people, Israel. Moses, too, it is sometimes asserted, never existed; not to mention Adam and Eve. The stories *are* filled with obvious mythological touches, and one can never know where historical truth leaves off and mythology begins.

These issues are all important for Biblical scholarship, but

they will not concern us in this book, for it is the story itself
with which we are concerned. And so, in retelling these tales,
I have taken them as they stand—neither questioning their historicity nor credibility, but focusing upon them purely as stories.
For, from the psychological point of view, it makes no more
difference whether Jacob existed than it does whether or not
Shakespeare's Hamlet existed, or Jesus' Prodigal Son. It is the
story of what happened to them that counts, which carries
its own message. So we will not "fight" the story, but will
try to listen so fully to it that its deeper meaning and implications
may be revealed to us.

We can be sure that questions of historicity and credibility
did not trouble the ancient Hebrews who first told and listened
to these tales. For them, these ancient stories became part of
the fabric of their souls, affecting them at a deep level of their
being; sacred tales to be preserved for all time. When stories
do this, it is because they bear an unconscious, as well as
a conscious, meaning. This happens whenever a story is archetypal, that is, when it carries within it a meaning which
is typical for all mankind. Mythology, fairy tales and the ancient
stories from the Bible are all archetypal; they have a power
to affect us through the unconscious by stimulating and arousing
in us the living imagery of the soul. These stories have power
because they tell how it always has been and always will be
with man. That being so, they affect us, even when they are
not rationally understood. In this book I will try to draw out
the inner meaning of the story, illuminating it with a running
psychological commentary. This is necessary for many modern
readers if we are to get into the tales personally. Of course,
for the ancient Hebrews, the stories probably affected them
on such a deep, non-rational level that a psychological commentary was not necessary at all.

I have selected these particular stories because they concern
the most important and fundamental process which goes on
in human life: the transformation of human beings from egocentric, unconscious persons, to persons of wholeness, breadth
of vision, and spiritual awareness. The Swiss psychologist, C. G.
Jung, gave the name "individuation" to this process of inner
development. The stories of Jacob, Joseph, and Moses are per-

haps the first (and among the best) stories we have of individuation, of growth to wholeness and vision; and the tale of
Adam and Eve tells us in mythological form how it all began.
Since becoming a whole and conscious person is at the center
of the meaning of *our* lives as well, these stories will have
a vital message for us, too.

The plan of the book is simple. Each story is retold, and
some of its inner meaning is explored in the retelling. Since
the stories are presented from a psychological perspective, all
psychological terms used in the retelling will be explained as
the story progresses. No prior knowledge of psychology is necessary to read the book, or grasp its meaning for you. You
may wish to re-read the stories from the Bible first. A modern
translation, such as the Jerusalem Bible (which is used in this
book) is recommended. However, this is not necessary, since
the whole tale will be recapitulated as we go. Logically enough,
the stories of Jacob, Joseph and Moses come in historical order.
Not so logically, the story of Adam and Eve is last, because
the meaning in this story becomes clearer *after* the message
of the others has been digested.

So the curtain goes up, the dramatis personae are on stage,
and a part of the great Biblical drama of human existence
is about to begin again!

PART ONE

The Man
Who Wrestled
With God

CHAPTER ONE

Jacob's Cunning

Jacob's grandfather was Abraham, that sturdy and gifted man who heard God speaking with him in his dreams and visions. It was because of God's Voice that Abraham left his home in the civilized city of Ur in Mesopotamia and made the long journey to the unknown land of Canaan, there to begin the epic story of the Hebrew people.

Jacob's father was Isaac. As a boy Isaac was almost sacrificed by Abraham, who thought it was God's Will that this be done. At the last moment, God spoke to Abraham and told him that it was not required that Isaac be sacrificed to Him; Abraham found a ram caught in a nearby bush and used the animal as a sacrifice instead. No doubt this story has a lot to do with the elimination of human sacrifice from the rites of the Hebrew people at a time when it was prevalent among the Semitic people roundabout, but it also suggests that Isaac may have been so badly frightened by God that for the rest of his life he kept Him at a distance. At any rate, unlike his father Abraham, Isaac apparently had no direct relationship with God. There were no dreams or visions, no voice which spoke to Isaac. Isaac worshipped Yahweh reverently and faithfully, but indirectly, by maintaining a tradition about Him. Of all the patriarchs of the Hebrews he was the least gifted spiri-

tually. He was an honest man, and no great fault can be found
in him, but neither was there any brilliance. The world is full
of Isaacs. We need them and they are good people, but they
are not used by God to further the development of human
consciousness in the manner of men like Abraham.

The best thing Isaac did was to marry Rebekah. Rebekah
was as original and gifted as Isaac was ordinary. The story
of Jacob rightfully begins with the story of Rebekah, a remarkable woman, whose consciousness and courage played a
crucial role in the life and development of her son.

Now Isaac and Rebekah had been married for some time
and still Rebekah had no children. In those days childbearing
was virtually the only way for a woman to fulfill herself. Not
to have children, especially sons, was a disaster, and so the
would-be parents prayed earnestly to Yahweh for help. In due
course Yahweh heard their prayer, and Rebekah became preg-
nant with not one child, but two. Rebekah must have been
overjoyed at first, but soon her joy turned to gloom as she
realized that the unborn twins were struggling together in her
womb. "If this is the way of it," she declared, "why go on
living?" (Gen. 25:23). Rebekah took the animosity of the unborn
children toward each other as an ill omen for the future; disaster,
not happiness, might be the outcome of her childbirth.

Some people when they are depressed just give up, or try
to drown their pain in something which will take it away,
but Rebekah was made of sterner stuff. She determined to find
out the meaning of it, and in this way she was able to cure
herself of her depression and find out the purpose of her life.
Her way of getting to the bottom of her depression was to
consult Yahweh.

We do not know exactly how she went about doing this.
Later in the Old Testament there are three established ways
of divining the Mind of God. One way was to cast the sacred
lots—the Urim and Thummim—and to read the Will of God
from the pattern of the lots. We find repeated examples of
this, for instance, in the story of Saul, David, and Jonathan.
In the Books of Samuel no serious action is undertaken without
consulting the Divine Mind first, and the casting of the sacred

lots was the usual method. We may smile at this quaint notion of how God's Will may be determined, yet as late as the Book of Acts, when the disciples must choose a replacement for Judas, we find the same method is used. There is also the example of the Chinese Oracle book, the I Ching, in which a method for divining the Will of Heaven through the casting of lots has been devised which is remarkable for its wisdom and profundity. The other Old Testament means of ascertaining the Will of God were through dreams and through consulting a prophet, who might have dreams for you.

There are crucial times in our lives when it is of great importance that our actions and attitudes be in accordance with the Divine Will, and Rebekah was right in following her instincts and going to "consult Yahweh." The answer Rebekah got from God was surprising; she learned something which would never have occurred to her. God proclaimed to her:

"There are two nations in your womb,
Your issue will be two rival peoples.
One nation shall have the mastery of the other,
And the elder shall serve the younger." (Gen. 25:23)

Rebekah never forgot what God had told her. From this time on she did everything in her power to help Jacob, the second of the twins to be born, to supplant his brother Esau as the family patriarch. For in those days the oldest male of the clan was the leader of the family, with both temporal and spiritual authority. The family clan at that time was the basic social unit. Social functions which in our day are carried out by institutions, such as education, justice, war, police, caring for the ill, in that time were functions of the clan. At the head of the clan was the oldest male, the patriarch, to be succeeded at his death by the oldest son. So the patriarch was like a miniature king, ruling over his own small kingdom. Tradition had established that the oldest son would succeed his father, but Rebekah decided to act against tradition. Because of the oracle she had received, she was convinced that divine destiny was calling Jacob, not Esau, to the position of preeminence. Rebekah bore the burden of a secret knowledge and conviction, and began to carry out a plan in which others could not share.

As soon as the two boys were born, it was apparent that they were going to be very different people. Esau is described as a hairy person, and Jacob as smooth-skinned, suggesting at once that they have opposite natures. Esau became a man of the outdoors, of the field and earth, physically robust and active, a sort of super-masculine character. He thought in a literal, down-to-earth kind of way, like his father, and was very concerned with his immediate environment, having a "what's-for-dinner?" kind of mentality. Inevitably he became his father's favorite. Jacob became an inward-looking man, who stayed at home in his mother's tents, a mother's boy who spent much time with his own thoughts and fantasies.

He became Rebekah's favorite, not only because of the secret ambitions she cherished for him, but because they shared the same kind of soul.

In the language of psychology, Esau seems to have been the extravert, and Jacob the introvert; the former was oriented to the outer world, and the latter to the inner world. Esau was also a sensation type of person, a person who is aware of the immediate environment around him, but Jacob was an intuitive person, aware of the possibilities in life. Thus Esau could overlook the value of his birthright with all of the possibilities it might bring him in life, but the intuitive Jacob, left to his own thoughts in his mother's tents, developed the fantasy that he, rather than Esau, should have the legacy of his father. Esau was much too engrossed in the business of hunting to be aware of his fantasies, but Jacob lived very much within the life of his imagination, and out of his heart came the dream that he should have the family power. But how was he to get it? The fulfilment of his ambition gripped the young Jacob's mind, even as the fulfilment of divine prophecy absorbed the mind of his mother.

His mother's hopes for him were rooted in divine prophecy, but there was nothing sacred about Jacob's ambitions. Jacob, as his mother's favorite, was a young man with a first-rate mother complex, the kind of mother complex which leads to a particularly virulent form of egocentricity. The boy who is the center of his mother's world also fancies himself as the center of the universe. Rebekah's love for Jacob gave to his personality a fundamental reservoir of psychological strength which later on stood him in good stead. A person who has been loved as a child has a core of emotional reserve and strength which is irreplaceable. But there was also an overlay of selfishness and ruthlessness in Jacob's character. His ambition to become the ruler of his family was a naked desire for personal power and dominance; there was nothing spiritual or religious about it. In contrast, Esau seems free of this kind of ruthless egocentricity, and one wonders why God chose Jacob, rather than Esau, to carry on the family's spiritual inheritance. But at least Jacob knew what he wanted from life, while Esau was content to just take life as it came along.

One day the moment came for which Jacob had been waiting. Esau arrived home from hunting in a famished condition, and Jacob, who doubtless had been home all day taking it easy, was stirring some hot lentil soup. "Let me eat the red soup, that red soup there," said Esau. "I am exhausted." But Jacob said cunningly, "First sell me your birthright, then." Jacob did not hesitate to take advantage of Esau's weakness of character, nor to make capital on the great extremity in which Esau found himself, and Esau gave in. "Here I am, at death's door," Esau said; "what use will my birthright be to me?" Jacob made him cement the bargain with an unbreakable oath, and then gave him the soup in exchange for the coveted birthright. (Gen. 25:30-34).

Most of us who are raised in the Judeo-Christian ethic try to live life in the right way. We believe it is better to be honest, fair, open, and loving, rather than ruthless and cheating. So we strive to fulfil an ideal of honesty, or at least to appear to people as a person who cares, and who would not stoop to lying and cheating. But there is always the other one in us, the one who would lie and cheat, who does not care about others, but is selfish and grasping. We may try to live by the Ten Commandments, but we must remember that these commandments would not be necessary if there was not a tendency in all of us to break them; that is, to kill, to cheat, to covet, to steal. This other, darker personality within us we can call the "shadow."[1] We all have a shadow personality, a side of ourselves which contradicts our ego ideal of what we ought to be or want to be. What makes Jacob different is that he unashamedly identifies with what, for most of us, would be our shadow personality. Without batting an eye he sets out to get what he wants for himself, and is ruthless with Esau without, apparently, a moment of guilt.

On the other hand, Esau also has a shadow. Jacob's shadow is active—he sets out to get something even though it means defying the customary mores of society and relationship. Esau's shadow is a passive shadow—he gives in to his weakness. That he felt guilty about giving away his birthright for a bowl of soup is suggested by his rationalization: "Here I am, at death's door; what use will my birthright be to me?" Esau persuaded himself that he was starving to death and had no choice, but actually it takes a long time to starve to death. He was not at death's door; he was only a very hungry man without the spiritual strength and sense of value to endure his hunger a little longer for the sake of preserving his spiritual birthright. The shadow is not only what we do, it is also what we do not do; it is not only our ruthlessness, it is also our weakness. That the authors of our story saw this, and were not sympathetic to Esau, is shown in the final statement about this incident: "That was all Esau cared for his birthright." (Gen. 25:30).

So Jacob won from his brother the coveted birthright, but there was something even more important which Jacob needed if he was to complete his plan: he must secure his father's blessing. Just before the patriarch died he gave a blessing to the son who would succeed him. This blessing conveyed a tangible power and potency and, once given, could not be taken back. Since Jacob and Rebekah knew that Isaac would give this blessing to his favorite and elder son, Esau, it was necessary to deceive the old man into giving it to Jacob instead, a task made possible because Isaac was now blind.

This time Rebekah is the central figure in the story. The betrayal of her husband and one of her sons is certainly an

---

[1]To use the term coined for our dark inner adversary by C. G. Jung.

offense against generally accepted standards of morality. Looked at from a conventional point of view, Rebekah is a dreadful woman who stops at nothing to achieve her ends, and breaks the sacred trust relationship between a husband and wife. But there are important considerations which make Rebekah's case unique. What Rebekah is trying to bring about is not for herself, nor even for her favorite son, Jacob, but for God. Had Rebekah placed upon Jacob her own unrealized ambitions, she would have ruined him completely. A son who carries his mother's ambitions is also destroyed by them. Usually he is forced by life to be a failure, for this is the only way he can become free of her domination and find something of his own personality. Fortunately for Jacob it is not Rebekah's personal ambition for him which is involved here, but her inner conviction that this is God's plan.

But could she not have left it up to God to bring about Jacob's supremacy if that is what He wanted? Perhaps, but God also seems to work through people. It may be that without Rebekah's consciousness and sense of purpose the destiny stored up for Jacob would never have been realized. Then divine destiny would have had to wait for another day, and a more dedicated person to help carry it out, before it was fulfilled.

Rebekah's unusual motive for her actions makes it possible for her to forsake what has been called the ethic of obedience for the ethic of creativity.[2] The ethic of obedience requires us to follow the commonly accepted standards of human conduct and relationship. Most of us do well to live within a moral code of this kind, which has been tested throughout the centuries and embodies the usual rules of human decency. But there is also an ethic of creativity which requires us to be guided by our own inner truth. Then we do what we feel we must even though it runs counter to what is usually accepted. A person who departs from the usually accepted standards of behavior puts himself in a perilous position. It is all too easy to fall into the trap of simply justifying the means by the end,

---

[2]These terms were originally coined, as far as I know, by the Russian religious philosopher Nicholas Berdyaev. I have given them a psychological meaning in my book *The Kingdom Within*, J. B. Lippincott Co., p. 67.

and deluding oneself that since the goal of our behavior was (in our minds) divinely sanctioned, the ends we chose were justified. All too readily this pose is simply another mask behind which to hide our selfish motives. Only a very psychologically aware person, who truly knows himself and especially his power motives, and is genuinely in touch with the divine purpose, can successfully follow the ethic of creativity. Only if a person knows what he is doing, accepts responsibility for what he is doing, and has come to terms with his egocentricity so that his goals are not self-serving, can he depart from the ethic of obedience and follow the ethic of creativity. But when this does occur, the highest and most moral life of all is lived.

The key to a moral life founded upon inner truth is psychological honesty and knowledge of one's true motives. Jesus gives us a good example of this in a saying which is found in many ancient manuscripts following Luke 6:5. According to this story, Jesus sees a man working on the Sabbath Day, thereby defying custom and breaking the established Jewish mores. "Friend," he says to him, "if you know what you are doing, you are blessed; but if you do not know, you are accursed as a breaker of the Law." Rebekah knows what she is doing. She *is* breaking the usual laws of human behavior when she schemes to betray her husband and elder son, but she is fulfilling a higher law as she follows what she knows is the Divine Will. There are no personal rewards for her actions. No doubt she alienated completely the affections of Isaac and Esau, and her actions led to the exile of Jacob, whom she never saw again. The divine guidance she felt she was following, given her from the oracle perhaps twenty years earlier, was something she could not share with anyone. She had to act out of extreme loneliness and pain, and that takes great psychological strength. All of this marks Rebekah as an unusually conscious woman of remarkable psychological development and spiritual depth. At this point she is the only conscious person in our story.

Jacob is also going to serve divine destiny in the act of deception which is shortly to take place. By stealing his father's blessing from Esau, Jacob paves the way for the fulfilment of a divine purpose. But Jacob's motives for doing this are egocentric power motives; he is totally unaware of divine destiny at work. Because he is an egocentric and unconscious person, he must pay a big price later on for his actions. Everything we do unconsciously, without awareness of our motives and without moral reflection, we must pay for later on. But the paradox is that the sin against the collective moral standards had to take place. It was a stupid tradition which decreed that spiritual authority should be passed on to the eldest son, rather than the one most spiritually suited for it. Quite often a departure from usual morality must take place when God's purposes are to be served, or when an individual is to reach a greater psychological development; yet a person who does this without knowing what he is doing must pay the price for it. As we shall see, Jacob paid a big price indeed.

One day the blind old Isaac declared to Esau: "My son! See, I am old and do not know when I may die. Now take your weapons, your quiver and bow; go out into the country and hunt me some game. Make me the kind of savoury I like and bring it to me, so that I may eat, and give you my blessing before I die." (Gen. 27:1-4). The story tells us that Rebekah "happened to be listening" while Isaac was saying these things to Esau. We suspect that it was no coincidence that she overheard these words of Isaac to Esau, and that this is the moment for which she had been waiting for a long time, the moment when the all-important blessing will be bestowed. Rebekah has a plan already devised for the occasion. Summoning Jacob, she tells him to bring her a kid from the flocks which she will then prepare into the kind of savoury food which Isaac likes. Then Jacob is to take the food to his father and pass himself off as Esau and in this way secure the family blessing.

Jacob has a few qualms about this scheme, but they are qualms for his safety, not qualms of conscience. He says, "If my father happens to touch me, he will see I am cheating him, and I shall bring down a curse on myself instead of a blessing." (Gen. 27:12). But Rebekah is already prepared for this possibility and tells him to cover his smooth skin with the hairy skin of the slain kid.

Next comes a tale of blatant deception as Jacob goes to his father and tells him a series of bald-faced lies. (Gen. 27:18-27).

When Isaac asks who is there Jacob answers: "I am Esau your first-born." When Isaac wants to know how he got the game so quickly, Jacob is forced to tell a second lie to back up the first one, and invokes the name of Yahweh for his purposes, replying: "It was Yahweh your God who put it in my path." Notice that Jacob says *your* God; at this point Jacob has no God of his own, his only god is himself. After a few more lies (it always takes a string of lies to back up the first one), Jacob gets what he wants and the old man gives him his irrevocable blessing.

Jacob departs, and soon Esau comes back. There follows a heart-rending scene as the deception is discovered and the anguished Esau begs his father to give him a blessing too. But there is nothing that can be done; the blessing has been given to Jacob and cannot be taken back. Jacob has supplanted his brother.

So Jacob has secured for himself the spiritual legacy of the family, but he does not realize what he has done. He thinks he is simply getting the power and status of the family patriarch, but as the story unfolds he comes to realize, painfully and gradually, that in getting the spiritual legacy of the family he has been marked out by God. For God had spoken directly to Jacob's grandfather, Abraham, and made a personal covenant and relationship with him, and this personal relationship with God is what Jacob is acquiring for himself, though he does not know it yet. From this time on Jacob is a marked man in God's eyes, and as a result of this he will be forced to undergo great changes in his character. A process of development will be forced upon the unsuspecting Jacob which will compel him to become a conscious, moral and whole person. The developmental process which takes place in Jacob is the focal point of the entire story.

But why should God have chosen the wily Jacob for this unique relationship? Perhaps because Jacob possessed that particular quality, mentioned earlier, which is indispensable for psychological and spiritual growth and development: he was psychologically honest. To be psychologically honest means that a person is capable of seeing the truth about himself and what he is doing. Jacob's psychological honesty appears when he expresses anxiety to his mother that his father will discover the deception. Says the anxious Jacob: "Look, my brother Esau is hairy, while I am smooth-skinned. If my father happens to touch me, he will see *I am cheating him,* and I shall bring down a curse on myself instead of a blessing." Jacob does not disguise from himself what he is doing: he is cheating his father.

Most of us hide our duplicity from ourselves by using euphemisms instead of the real words for things we cannot face up to e.g., instead of "dying," people "pass away," suggesting that death is something we are unable to look at. Instead of facing up to what we are doing we rationalize our behavior, as we saw Esau doing when he gave up his birthright for a bowl of soup. But there is no rationalization with Jacob. He is going to cheat his father and he is perfectly frank about this with himself. He calls a spade a spade, and this quality of psychological honesty is of fundamental importance to spiritual and psychological development. Without it nothing can take place; with it there is always the possibility that God, Who psychologically speaking is the urge toward wholeness, can break through our egocentricity and make something of us. How God now breaks through Jacob's egocentricity and makes of him a fitting instrument to carry out the spiritual legacy of his people makes up the rest of our narrative.

CHAPTER TWO

Jacob's Transformation

An egocentric person tries to make life revolve around himself. He puts himself in the center of life and expects life to serve and gratify him, instead of being willing to be the servant of life. He worships himself and acknowledges no greater authority in his life than his own wants. The egocentric person strives to control and manipulate his environment, especially others around him. If he is successful he may appear to be strong, but it is a demonic kind of power, not to be confused with true ego strength. The person with true ego strength can afford to give up his egocentricity; the person with a weak ego falls back upon manipulative devices to maintain his sense of power.

Fritz Kunkel[1] used to speak of four typical egocentric types: the Star, the Clinging Vine, the Turtle, and the Nero. The Star maintains his egocentricity by seeking the limelight, adulation and glory; stars love to shine. The egocentricity of the Clinging Vine takes a very different form, for this person often seems to strike a humble pose, but the clinging, overly dependent attitude of such a person is an egocentric attempt to avoid a responsible life. This person's life adaptation is basically parasitical. The Turtle's great problem is relating to people, and

---

[1]Fritz Kunkel outlined these four types of egocentricity in his book *How Character Develops.* Cf. his *In Search of Maturity* and *Creation Continues.*

20

his egocentric defense is to pull inside a shell so no one can reach him. His egocentricity takes the form of hiding from life and relationships, living encased in psychological armor. The Nero's egocentricity takes the form of a lust for direct power and control. This kind of person wants to dominate, and this is the form of egocentricity which characterized the young Jacob.

There are three basic experiences in which our egocentricity can be changed: through suffering, through the recognition of a power greater than our own will at work in our lives, and by coming to care for someone other than ourself. All three of these experiences now come to Jacob in quick succession, as though his egocentricity was so strong that a powerful dose of medicine was necessary to cure him. But the cure for egocentricity *is* strong medicine; unless we develop the right attitude such a medicine may kill us rather than cure us.

The first experience which comes to Jacob is suffering. So far Jacob has been able to avoid suffering. He hasn't even risked physical privation, letting Esau be the hunter in the wilderness while he stayed safely at home in his mother's tents. But when Jacob robs Esau of his father's blessing, Esau becomes furiously angry and determines to murder him. "The time to mourn for my father will soon be here. Then I will kill my brother, Jacob" he declares. (Gen. 27:41). Rebekah, who had her spies everywhere in the household, is told of what Esau has said, and admonishes Jacob to flee through the wilderness to the land of his Uncle Laban in far away Haran. Apparently Rebekah had been expecting this to happen and had a plan in mind to ensure Jacob's safety, but for Jacob it came as an unpleasant surprise. After all, when Jacob took Esau's birthright he did not run into this kind of anger, and perhaps Jacob expected the same kind of passivity on Esau's part when he took his blessing from him. But the first time Esau had been taken advantage of he had not expressed his anger because he felt too guilty; he was probably too ashamed to even let anyone know what had happened, for he knew in his heart that he had given in to weakness. However, this time Esau is without guilt and his anger is great, doubly so, perhaps, because he also remembers the first offense against him.

Jacob's failure to take into account Esau's anger plunged him into desperate straits. So far Jacob had never come up against a situation he could not manipulate to his own advantage, and, in addition, he had always been able to depend on the intercession and protection of his mother. But now something has gone seriously wrong.

So Jacob flees into the wilderness, an exile. A little later we will find Jacob makes a kind of prayer in which he bargains with God, and from the content of that prayer we know that Jacob feared for his life in this journey through the wilderness. It was not a journey to be taken lightly, especially for someone like Jacob who was not used to the wilds. Jacob, the introverted intuitive person, was ill-equipped to deal with the rigors of the unfamiliar environment of the wilderness. He was plunged into circumstances in which his highly developed side was useless, and he had to rely on undeveloped psychological functions. He could easily have perished from hunger or cold, been killed by bandits or wild animals, or lost his way and wandered hopelessly. So his journey into the wilderness was frightening and painful, and this time there was no way to avoid it.

To be forced to undergo a journey through the wilderness is an archetypal experience. Perhaps everyone who is called upon to a higher psychological development must undergo such a wilderness experience. There are many ways we are forced to undertake such a journey. People can be plunged into a psychological wilderness, a dreadful time of doubt, anxiety, or depression, and never leave their doorstep. Looked at purely clinically, the journey through the wilderness appears to be a sickness or breakdown; looked at spiritually, it may be an initiation or rite-of-passage we must undergo in order that a change in consciousness may be brought about. Egocentricity dies hard in most of us. Often only the pain of a wilderness journey can bring about the desired new attitude.

But an egocentric person can cheat even at suffering. Caught in our wilderness experience, with its pain and confusion, many of us try to turn our pain into self-pity, or use our suffering to play the martyr role and manipulate others, or perhaps just give up in the face of the pain and want to die. Suffering by itself is no cure, it only cures us when we have the right attitude toward it. Perhaps Jacob's psychological honesty stood him in good stead here. We have seen that he was not a person to rationalize, and perhaps in this wilderness he faced his pain and realized that he had brought it upon himself. At any rate, as we shall see, the Jacob who emerges from the wilderness in the land of Haran is not the same person who entered it.

The second experience which breaks down Jacob's egocentricity is his encounter with a Will greater than his own which breaks in upon him in his famous dream. Far out in the wilderness, frightened and alone, Jacob lies down in exhaustion to sleep, resting his head upon a rock for a pillow. In the depths of the night Jacob is shocked by a numinous dream in which he sees a great ladder reaching from earth to heaven, with angels ascending and descending upon it, and from the heavens God's Voice speaks to him: "I am Yahweh, the God of Abraham your father, and the God of Isaac." (Gen. 28:13). Jacob awakes in great fear from this nightmarish experience. "How awe-inspiring this place is!" he exclaims. "This is nothing less than a house of God; this is the gate of heaven!" (Gen. 28:17).

As I have shown in my book *Dreams: God's Forgotten Language,*[2] dreams and their companion experience, visions, are regarded in the Bible as the way par excellence in which God speaks to man. From the Book of Genesis through the Book of Revelation, the Divine breaks in upon man through startling dreams. The dreams of the Bible have long been disregarded by the Church and theology, but in our time the discoveries of depth psychology are supporting the ancient conviction of the men of the Bible that in the experience of the dream man is in touch with a meaning beyond himself. Jacob's dream is typical of the numinosity of Biblical dream experiences.

The words "numinous" and "numinosum" come from the Latin word "numen", which means a presiding spirit or divine being, and a numinous experience occurs when we are confronted

---

[2] *Dreams: God's Forgotten Language,* Chapter VI; J. B., Lippincott Company, 1968; also see Morton T. Kelsey's *Dreams: The Dark Speech of the Spirit* (later published as *God, Dreams and Revelation*) for a full treatment of the role of dreams in the Christian tradition.

by an autonomous spiritual power. If, for instance, you enter your house at night, the lights fail to turn on when you throw the switch, there is an eery chill in the air, and you then see a weird ball of light moving through the air and hear the sound of a chain clanking in the attic, you are having a numinous experience. That could be called an experience of negative numinosity, since the spiritual being you are confronting is a ghost. (I am not asking the reader to believe in ghosts, but only illustrating what a numinous experience is like.)

But even an experience with a positive numinous power is frightening. Professor Rudolph Otto, who in his book, *The Idea of the Holy,* first coined the words numinous and numinosum, pointed out that a numinous experience always inspires in us awe, fear, and a sense of what he called our "creatureliness" (our mortality and finitude). He also showed that numinosity is the main attribute of God in the Bible; His holiness lies in His numinosity, so that we can call God the "Numinosum," that is, the source of the numinous experience. Later, C. G. Jung used the term numinous because he found that many experiences with the unconscious had this quality, that the center of the unconscious was a powerful numinosum, and that many modern dreams, like Biblical dreams, have numinous effects upon consciousness.

In his dream Jacob experiences this Numinosum, and instinctively Jacob, who, as we noted earlier, had no belief in God, now recognizes that God has spoken to him. For the first time in his life he is forced to recognize the existence of a Will greater than that of his own ego. Jacob has a primitive kind of psychology, and at this point decides that he had such a dream because God was in that particular spot. When he leaves he erects a small stone altar there to mark this as a numinous place. It was common among the ancients to suppose that certain places on the earth were unusually numinous. Yahweh, for instance, dwelt in a special way on Mt. Sinai; in the Greek world, Asklepius could be sought out at certain springs and fountains; and Apollo spoke at Delphi where the earth had a great fissure. Even today we have the healing power at Lourdes, and many suppose that the altar in a church carries a special charge of the sacred, numinous power. There may, in fact, be something to the idea that certain places are especially numinous, but later Jacob will come to realize that God is no respecter of places, and can appear to him in a psychological way, not being dependent on a particular geographical location.

Jacob's first attempt to relate to this newly discovered Power which spoke to him in his dream is also awkward. Jacob's son, Joseph, was at home with dreams and a master interpreter of them, but Jacob is basically a man of practical reality and worldly affairs. His reaction to the dream is tinged with his practical side and with his egocentric leanings, as he tries to make a deal with God. In this bargain Jacob tries to strike with Yahweh, we can see how frightened he was on his wilderness journey: "If God goes with me," he declares, "and keeps me safe on this journey I am making, if he gives me bread to eat and clothes to wear, and if I return home safely to my father, then Yahweh shall be my God." (Gen. 28:20-22). This is a pretty crass bargain Jacob tries to strike with God, and shows where his spiritual development is at this point. It reminds us of many people today whose religious outlook is much the same—if God takes care of me and no adversity crosses my path, I will go to Church and make the proper religious observances. Nevertheless, Jacob has found himself compelled to take into account this God Whom he has not known before. For Jacob, this bargain is religious progress. Another Will than his own has been acknowledged, and so a small but significant dent has been made in his egocentric attitude.

It is interesting that Jacob's dream can be interpreted in the light of modern dream psychology. In interpreting a dream we rely on three sources of information: First, we need to know about the dreamer and his own particular life situation, for, as a general rule, dreams are highly individual; they belong to us, and no one else. Secondly, we need to know the associations the dreamer has to the symbols and events of his dream; that is, what the symbols, persons, or events in his dream make him think of. Third, we may need to draw upon our knowledge of the symbols and motifs found in the mythologies and religions of the world in order to understand certain types of dreams which come from that area of the psyche which is called the "collective unconscious".[3]

In Jacob's case we do know a great deal about his personal life circumstances when he had this dream, especially that the dream occurred at a time of great psychological crisis when his world seemed to be collapsing around him. We also have some of Jacob's personal associations to the dream, since it is clear that the dream made him think immediately of Yahweh, the Divine Being of Whom his father had often spoken, but Whose existence he had hitherto denied, or at least ignored as far as his own life was concerned. Finally, because it is a very numinous dream, it is evident that it is an archetypal one, which comes from the great storehouse of mythological and religious symbols deep within the unconscious.

For there are striking parallels between Jacob's dream and the lore of shamanism. The shaman, or medicine man as the white man calls him, is the ancient American Indian or Asian healer. He was a primitive priest, educator, and doctor rolled into one. Mircea Eliade, in his book on the subject,[4] has shown that shamanic lore is much the same the world over. How a young man is called to be a shaman, is trained in his profession, how he performs his cures, and the cosmological outlook he holds, are universal.

According to the shamanistic world view there are three planes of reality: the earthly world, the underworld below, and the celestial world above. Ordinary men live only on the central or earth plane of reality and know little or nothing of the worlds above and below. These other worlds are the realms of the gods and demons, of healing and sickness, of death and rebirth. What makes the shaman different from ordinary men is that he has been seized upon by the beings of the upper or lower regions and taken into their abode. Here he is shown the mysteries of illness and healing, life and death. This shamanic "call" is often brought to him in a vivid dream or vision,

---

[3]The collective unconscious is the term Jung gives to a psychic substratum which is the same in all men.

[4]Mircea Eliade, *Shamanism*—Princeton University Press.

such as those which came to the prophet Ezekiel, accompanied by an acute illness or psychological crisis. In this mind-altering experience, the shaman-to-be reports experiencing a journey to the upper or lower worlds where he comes to know the gods of sickness and healing, things which other men, without such an initiatory experience, cannot hope to know. The shaman reports his experience as though it happened to him physically. We would understand that he had a visionary journey through the unconscious, in which he came to know secrets of the psyche inaccessible to the uninitiated, and, by means of his experience, attained a greatly enlarged consciousness.

The shaman's journey to the upper or lower regions was possible because of a link which connected the sky, the earth, and the underworld, the location of which was revealed to the shaman in his experience. This link was represented in shamanic lore as a world pole, a cosmic tree at the center of the earth, a celestial rope, *or a ladder,* connecting heaven and earth. By means of this, one could ascend and descend to and from the upper and lower realms.

If we interpret Jacob's dream as a version of the worldwide shamanic type of initiation experience, we can make some hypotheses about its meaning. Jacob has the possibility of experiencing a new consciousness; that is, his conscious mind is now exposed to heaven. Psychologically this means that unknown contents of an illuminating, consciousness-expanding nature may now begin to enter his consciousness. When this happens, people become, as the shaman did, different from others around them. For such encounters with the unconscious are private, cannot be acquired collectively or through education, but can only come through personal psychological experience. They are the mark of the "twice born," and occur one way or another to all those who achieve a higher psychological and spiritual life.

The dream came to Jacob at this precise time because this is the moment of his own psychological crisis. Earlier, when everything was going for him as planned and expected, such an invitation to higher consciousness would not have been possible. It is only when the conscious point of view is severely shaken, through an illness, catastrophe, or some experience like

Jacob's, that such a contact with the spiritual side of the unconscious is possible.

It is worth noting, however, that in the dream Jacob did
not ascend the ladder; only the angels ascended and descended
upon it, while Jacob remained a passive observer of his own
dream. It is important to observe in our dreams the activity
or inactivity of the dream figure who represents the ego and
with whom we are identified. Often we are an active participant
in the action; sometimes we are just the passive recipient of
what happens to us; other times the action takes place all on
its own and we seem to be only an observer. So it was with
Jacob, and I think this shows that at this point in his development he is not yet conscious enough to make such an
ascent to heaven. Jacob has been too busy trying to get power
for himself over the things on earth to be prepared to make
this ascent. He does not yet even have enough curiosity about
the things of the Spirit to venture closer or to ask questions.

At long last Jacob emerges from the wilderness journey.
We may imagine his relief that he has arrived safely in a land
where there are other people and where he is beyond the dangers
of starvation or wandering lost in the unfamiliar, untracked
desert. He has been through a shocking experience, and has
been tested physically and psychologically. Not the least among
his frightening, transforming memories is his recollection of
the numinous Voice which spoke to him in his dream.

As he stumbles out of the desert wilderness he comes upon
a well, and gathered around it are shepherds with their flocks.
Jacob strikes up a conversation with them and learns that they
are from nearby Haran, so he knows he has arrived safely
at his destination. The shepherds are waiting until all the flocks
are gathered together, when they will roll the heavy stone from
the well and water all of the sheep together, but at this point
Rachel, the daughter of Jacob's Uncle Laban, arrives with her
father's sheep. Jacob, told by the shepherds who she is, goes
to the well, rolls back the heavy stone, and waters Rachel's
flock for her. It is the first time we read of Jacob's doing
anything for anyone else. The action is significant: a change
has taken place in this egocentric young man. Rachel runs
ahead to tell her father that Jacob has come, and Laban comes

to meet him. They embrace and Laban exclaims, in words which, as we will see later, have an ironic meaning, "Truly you are my bone and flesh!" (Gen. 29:14).

What now happens to Jacob is the third great event which shatters his egocentricity and paves the way for a larger life: he falls in love. It seems that Laban has two daughters. The elder is named Leah, but the story tells us that "there was no sparkle in Leah's eyes." Rachel, on the other hand, is described as "shapely and beautiful" and, the story goes on, "Jacob had fallen in love with Rachel." (Gen. 29:17).

The fact that Jacob could fall in love at all shows that a certain amount of psychological growth had taken place in him during his journey through the wilderness. So far the only woman in his life had been his mother. As long as a man remains in a state of psychological development in which his mother is the most important woman to him, he cannot mature as a man. A man's eros, his capacity for love and relatedness, must be freed from attachment to the mother, and able to reach out to a woman who is his contemporary; otherwise he remains a demanding, dependent, childish person.

The transition from the world of the mother to being a man who is related to the world in a mature way, and able to love a woman as his soul, is so important that primitive societies have initiation rituals to help the boy make the bridge from childhood to manhood. These rites of passage vary from place to place but always involve exposing the young man to hardship, suffering, and privation, throwing him, so to speak, on his own resources. Jacob's journey through the wilderness has evidently served as such a rite of passage. There was no mother there to help him in his dangerous wilderness journey; he had to rely upon himself, his own fortitude and desire to live. Jacob had to put to death his childish yearnings for comfort and security, and had taken on life as a man. In this way he was prepared for his great love affair with Rachel, and the image of woman he carried within his soul shifted from a mother-image to the image of woman as soul.

The love story between Jacob and Rachel is one of the great love stories of the Bible. Though Jacob had two wives and several concubines, it was Rachel whom he loved to the end of his life. When she died he grieved greatly and erected a monument to her memory. The two sons she bore him, Joseph and Benjamin, were his favorites, because they were the sons of his beloved Rachel.

So Jacob fell in love with Rachel, and apparently Rachel also loved Jacob, but in those days getting married was more complicated than it is today, and it was necessary for a prospective bridegroom to pay a father for the privilege of marrying his daughter. After all, a man could not be expected to spend all those years raising daughters without getting something in return for it! Jacob, of course, was penniless. So he and Laban agreed that he would work for Laban for seven years in order to win the right to marry Rachel.

Now sometimes when a man falls in love with a woman he is, in reality, only in love with himself. A man carries around within himself an image of woman, a soul-image of the feminine, so to speak. In the phenomenon known as falling in love this soul image is seen by the man, in projected form, in the woman whom he loves. He is accordingly fascinated by this woman, feels incomplete without her, and yearns to be with her. But unless he learns to know and love the actual woman herself, his feelings of love remain illusory and immature. Some men only want to be in love with a goddess; they want the euphoric feeling of "being in love," but are incapable of loving a real person. Being in love means being caught up in the beauty of the projected soul image; loving means knowing and appreciating a woman for herself. Unless the first stage, being in love, is succeeded by the second, a man's love remains self-centered, and is, in fact, only a variation of his mother complex, in which he expects a woman to gratify him and make him happy.

One way to tell whether a man truly loves a woman, or is only indulging himself in being-in-love, is if he is willing to work for her. The ancient custom in which the husband bought the right to marry a girl was psychologically healthy, for it could mean that he loved her enough to work for her.

Today we do not have such a custom, but there is the possibility that a man can work on the relationship with a woman, and this is a measure of his capacity for love. A man who is unwilling to work to develop the relationship psychologically with a woman, but only wants an unconscious, instinctual relationship, wants a woman to be just an extension of himself. Not having learned to love a woman for her own sake, he tries to fit her into a box of his own devising, and have her live within a bundle of unconscious expectations. He then sees the woman, not as a person in her own right, but as someone who is to make him happy, that is, as mother. If she disappoints him in this, he turns sour, and may punish her by having nothing to do with her.

Jacob was not such a man. His love for Rachel was of such a quality that he developed a differentiated eros, a unique capacity for psychological relatedness, and an appreciation of the feminine side of life. Perhaps this, more than anything else, served to break down his egocentricity, and paved the way for his inner development.

Seven years seems like a long time for a man to work for a woman, but our story tells us that "they seemed to him (Jacob) like a few days because he loved her so much." (Gen. 29:20). It is true that when life is flowing, and energy is pouring into consciousness as it does when we are in love, time seems to speed by. Only when life is not flowing, and our creative energy is blocked, does life become dull and boring, and time weighs heavily on our hands.

Finally the great day comes for the wedding. In those days it was the custom for the bride to be veiled on her wedding day, so when Jacob is married, his wife-to-be is concealed behind her heavy Oriental veil. Imagine Jacob's shock and dismay when he goes to consummate his marriage and discovers that he has married Leah, not Rachel. Wily Laban substituted his homely older daughter for the beautiful younger one.

Jacob, of course, is enraged, and accuses Laban of being a terrible trickster. Now we realize the significance of Laban's greeting to Jacob, "Truly you are my bone and flesh!" This Laban is a trickster, just as Jacob is a trickster. Apparently Jacob has managed to forget, however, about the tricks he pulled on Isaac and Esau, and can only think of the injustice done to him. Jacob has turned over a new leaf in life, he is now working as an honest man, but he has not yet faced up to the trickster side of himself or else he would not have been so indignant about the trick Laban pulled on him.

We are never so righteously indignant as when someone does to us what we do to others but with which we have not yet come to terms. Laban, confronted by the angry Jacob, merely shrugs his shoulders and says, "It is not the custom in our country to give the younger before the elder." (Gen. 29:26). In other words, Jacob should have known this would happen, taking into account what a wily person his uncle is. His lapse in consciousness let him in for a bad shock, but that is often what it takes to make us more conscious. Now the tables are turned on him, and Jacob knows what it is like to be deceived. Another step in the development of his consciousness takes place. Perhaps he even thought to himself, "This is how my father and my brother must have felt."

Laban, to show what a good-hearted fellow he really is, makes Jacob what he thinks is a generous offer: if Jacob will work for him another seven years, he may have the right to marry Rachel right away. It is, if you like, the first instance in history of buying on the installment plan! Jacob wants Rachel so much that he accepts. Now he has two wives, and another seven years of hard work ahead of him.

The story now goes into a charming, but meaningful, digression: the struggle between Leah and Rachel for Jacob's love. Jacob, naturally, is resentful of Leah, and has little or no affection for her. God, seeing her plight, opens her womb, while Rachel remains barren. Soon Leah bears Jacob four sons— Reuben, Simeon, Levi and Judah—while Rachel is childless. Ordinarily a woman who bore so many sons would have greatly pleased her husband, for, as we have seen, sons were highly prized in that patriarchal era, and a woman who gave birth to sons was admired and appreciated, but Jacob still loved Rachel. This distinguishes him again as a man of eros, for whom a woman was a person to love, and a companion for life, and not simply a mother to his children and an extension of his social power and influence.

But even lovers quarrel, and one day Rachel can stand her frustration no longer. "Give me children, or I shall die!" she cries out to her husband. Jacob retorts angrily, "Am I

in God's place? It is he who has refused you motherhood."
(Gen. 30:2). So Rachel resorts to a desperate measure and sends
in her slave-girl, Bilhah, to Jacob, for it was the custom that
if the wife sent in her slave girl to have intercourse with her
husband, the children resulting from the union would legally
be those of the wife. So Jacob slept with the slave-girl Bilhah,
and two more sons were born to him: Dan and Naphtali. Rachel
rejoiced over this and exclaimed, "I have fought God's fight
with my sister, and I have won." (Gen. 30:8). But in her heart
she must have known that it was not the same thing as if
she herself had borne Jacob's sons.

The score was now four to two, and Leah, seeing that
she had no more children, took her slave girl, Zilpah, and
gave her to Jacob as a wife. Jacob, who was certainly having
a good time with all of this, had two more sons by Zilpah,
Gad and Asher, putting Leah far ahead of Rachel once again.
But still Jacob did not love Leah and he ceased to sleep with
her, which weighed heavily on her heart. Then one day Leah's
son, Reuben, found some mandrakes, which were highly prized
as aphrodisiacs. Rachel begged Leah to give her some of the
mandrakes, but Leah scornfully rejected her request, declaring
that she already had her husband, so why did she also want
her mandrakes? So Rachel bargained with Leah: in exchange
for the mandrakes she would persuade Jacob to sleep with
her again. On the strength of this bargain Leah bore Jacob
two more sons, Issachar and Zebulun, and also one daughter,
Dinah.

The score now seemed overwhelmingly in Leah's favor,
but at just this point God took pity on Rachel and opened
her womb. To her great joy she gave birth to a son—Joseph.
"God has taken away my shame," she exulted. (Gen. 30-24).
Joseph, as we know, became a great and famous man, one
of the towering personalities of the Bible. The child born out
of the love match was more important than all the other sons
put together. But Rachel's joy was shortlived. A few years
after the birth of Joseph, she conceived again, but in giving
birth to Benjamin she died.

The grief-stricken Jacob erected a monument to her memory
on the present site of Bethlehem, the birthplace of Christ. The

love which Jacob had lavished on Rachel now went to her two sons, and Joseph and Benjamin became their father's favorites. Perhaps each time he looked into their eyes he saw the eyes of his beloved wife and partner.

There is a sense in which every man has a Rachel and a Leah within him. It is as though there is a pull within a man toward social conformity and adaptation to outer demands and expectations. Jacob had married Leah because it was the socially expected thing to do. He did not love her, but she was a part of his life, just as outer conformities are a part of life. But there is also the pull from within a man toward the things of the soul. The beautiful feminine image within a man which so draws and attracts him is like a magnet seeking to pull him into his own inner truth. The two conflict. Outer demands and inner demands are invariably at war. A weaker man, less true to his own feelings, gives up his Rachel side and lives only for Leah and the world of convention. But a man who is true to eros remains faithful to his soul; such a man can come to relate to his inner world.

When Jacob was not involved in the intrigues of his wives, he was hard at work with his flocks and herds and he became in time a very successful and wealthy man. Had Jacob lived today, he would not have been a priest or minister, but a businessman, perhaps a banker, a cattle rancher, or the executive of a large corporation. Jacob did not live in a constant relationship with God, as Joseph did, for instance, who followed the word of God in his dreams, or Moses, who walked and talked with God each day. These men were shamans and prophets, but Jacob was a man who went about the worldly business of making a living, until from time to time, God crossed his path and spoke to him in unmistakable ways.

After Jacob finished his fourteen years of servitude to Laban, he turned his energies to building his own fortune, and with his shrewdness and industry he did well. The same cleverness and cunning he had used to cheat Esau and Isaac he now used in a legitimate way to build up his flocks and herds. At this point Jacob is making what might be called the "proper use of the shadow." The cunning fellow who had cheated his own family now became a cunning, but legitimate, entrepreneur.

In fact, Jacob became so wealthy he incurred the anger and jealousy of Laban, and in the resulting argument found a way to get back at him for the deception his uncle had perpetrated on him at the time of his marriage.

Laban, hoping to curb Jacob's success, got him to agree that all the black sheep and all the spotted and speckled goats would be Jacob's wages for working for Laban, and the others would belong to Laban. But Laban had a trick up his sleeve, and before he turned his flocks over to his nephew he had all the black sheep and spotted or speckled goats removed from the flocks. But this time Jacob was too clever for Laban. Each time the sheep bred, Jacob held up something black in front of them, and each time the goats bred he held up branches peeled into stripes by removing strips of bark. As a result only black sheep and speckled goats were born. We may question the theory of genetics of the ancient Hebrews, but the story illustrates amusingly how clever and shrewd Jacob was in his worldly dealings. He had found a good way to put his former shadowy cleverness to work, and this time there is no reproach. Laban had asked for it, and our sympathies are entirely with Jacob. Yet, as it turned out, it was partly his very success which led to an experience even more frightening and dangerous than his journey through the wilderness.

CHAPTER THREE

A Wrestling Match
With God

When Laban's sons see that Jacob is outwitting their father, they are enraged and begin to plot against him. Jacob realizes that things between him and his uncle are "not as they had been," and that he must find a way to escape. At this point Yahweh speaks again to Jacob in a dream. "Go back to the land of your forefathers and to your kindred; and I will be with you," He commands. (Gen. 31:2-4).

God's command is ominous, for we must remember that this meant returning to the land of Esau and facing the prospect of revenge at the hands of his estranged brother. It was not a happy prospect which Jacob faced. To be sure, he had to leave Haran, but why return to the land of Esau? Why not go another direction and find a safe home?

Jacob, however, decides to obey the Divine Voice. His deepest instinct is that he must trust God's command no matter how great the dangers seem to be and Jacob is faithful to this instinct, even though he is not in a position to know what God has in mind. However, we are in a position to see why Jacob needed to return to the land of his origins. The whole of Jacob's life since he left his home has been a long process of coming to terms with himself, and the replacement of his egocentricity by a larger, God-given personality. But this developmental process cannot be completed unless Jacob returns to the land of his earlier misdeeds and confronts Esau. To be sure, Jacob has done well in the land of Laban, living an honest and valuable life, but he has not yet faced up to the person he had been as a youth, nor has he made amends for the terrible things he did to his brother. His spiritual development cannot be complete until he is reconciled with Esau, and has faced and taken responsibility for the deceitful person he has been in the past.

But this is a dreadful task to have laid upon him. How much easier it would have been if God had been willing to settle for something less than a full accounting of his life, had allowed Jacob to spend his final years in peace and quiet. But God has no intention of letting Jacob alone until the final psychological truths and spiritual tasks have been realized. Now Jacob is learning what it meant to have the birthright of his people. This direct, confronting, demanding relationship with God *is* the birthright which Jacob, unknowingly, secured for himself. Like Abraham, his grandfather, who, at God's command left his comfortable home in Ur for the unknown wilderness of Canaan, so Jacob must now leave all security behind him, and face an unknown and dangerous future. Jacob who had originally sought the birthright to use for his own personal power purposes, finds he is used instead by a Power beyond himself.

So Jacob picks up his family, his flocks and herds and servants, and sets out for the land of Canaan. When he originally left Canaan he was a young man who followed his own will; now, as he returns, he is a man who is following a Will other than his own. Before, he only pursued goals he set up for himself; now he follows goals set up by God, goals which he would rather not pursue because they lead him into danger and uncertainty. This is how much he has changed, the extent to which his egocentricity has been replaced, and his personality reorganized around another center.

The story now rushes on to its climax. Jacob's wives go with him, their love for Jacob being stronger than their loyalty to their father. Laban pursues and overtakes them, but is led to recognize that Jacob is being guided by God; the two reach an agreement and become friends again. Laban returns home, and Jacob continues on his way until he reaches the stream Jabbok, on the other side of which lies the land of Canaan. Here he learns that Esau is coming to meet him. Jacob sends scouts ahead to give Esau a message of reconciliation, but the scouts see that Esau has four hundred fighting men with him. Filled with apprehension, they return to Jacob without having spoken to Esau, bringing with them the gloomy news that Esau approaches with armed soldiers.

Jacob shows us again how far he has departed from his egocentricity. Self-preservation would call for flight, but Jacob remains both obedient to his inner voice and solicitous over the welfare of his family and servants. In his extremity he prays, and his prayer this time is far different from the crude bargain he tried to strike with God after his dream in the middle of the wilderness. First Jacob thanks God for all the blessings given to him, and expresses his feeling of unworthiness for all of God's kindness. Then he reminds God of His promises to him, that He said He would guard and protect him. Finally he implores God to save him from Esau's wrath, and freely expresses his fear for himself and his family.

Jacob's prayer is open and honest. He lets his emotions come out in his prayer; no pious platitudes here, but an honest baring of his soul, and an open dialogue with God. Too many prayers fail to reach their mark because people do not pray with emotional honesty. Jacob shows us how to pray. If we are angry with God, say so; if we love Him, say so; if we are afraid, bring this into our prayer. Prayer is relationship with God and no relationship, certainly not with the Divine, exists without emotional honesty. Then, having done all he could in prayer, Jacob does what he can on his own. He divides his family, servants, and flocks into two companies and sends them on ahead by different routes, reasoning that if Esau falls upon one company and destroys it the other will still be safe. He himself remains alone that night in the camp.

There are some key experiences which come to us when we are with other people, and some which come to us only when we are alone. When we are alone it is as though the threshold of consciousness is lowered and powerful inner experiences can cross over into consciousness which would be screened out if our attention were diverted. So from time immemorial, men looking for the Spirit have sought solitude. Elijah, exiled by Queen Jezebel and defeated in spirit, journeyed alone to Mt. Horeb. Jesus, overburdened by his mission to the multitudes, retired to the desert to be alone. St. Augustine was converted alone in his garden. The young Indian brave went off alone into the wilderness to await his "big" dream in which a spiritual being would adopt him as his son, and this would be his entry into the world of manhood. Many people do not have such experiences because they are afraid to be alone. Today we turn on the radio or TV, or get on the phone to talk to our neighbor; anything to avoid that dread aloneness in which the Spirit may trouble us. Being alone takes spiritual courage, but this is a quality which Jacob possesses. It is another aspect of his psychological honesty, of which we spoke earlier.

Now we come to the strangest part of our story. While Jacob was alone at night by the side of the stream Jabbok, a being suddenly leaped on him. The Bible simply says, "And there was one" (Gen. 32:26) who wrestled with him until daybreak. Some kind of spiritual power, a seeming adversary, suddenly seized Jacob and wrestled with him in the darkness. We must use our imagination to realize what great psychological strength and spiritual courage it took for Jacob to wrestle with his nightmarish adversary throughout that long night, for this was no ordinary mortal who struggled with him, but a numinous being from the Unknown. A lesser man than Jacob might have died of fright, or pleaded for mercy, or tried to flee, but Jacob hung on, and all night long the two of them struggled together.

Finally the day began to dawn, and his adversary wanted to break off the struggle. Evidently it was the kind of spiritual encounter which vanishes with the light of day, for it is a fact that our minds are different at night, closer to a primitive level, and there are psychological experiences which occur in the darkness, but vanish with the dawn. But Jacob had not gone through this agony for nothing, and he refused to give up the struggle until he found out what it meant. "I will not let you go unless you bless me," Jacob declared to his numinous antagonist. (Gen. 32:27).

Jacob refused to part with his experience until he knew its meaning, and this marked him as a man of spiritual greatness. Everyone who wrestles with his spiritual and psychological experience, and, no matter how dark or frightening it is, refuses to let it go until he discovers its meaning, is having something of the Jacob experience. Such a person can come through his dark struggle to the other side reborn, but one who retreats or runs from his encounter with spiritual reality cannot be transformed.

The Divine Adversary replied to Jacob's demand with a question, "What is your name?" Then he added, "Your name shall no longer be Jacob, but Israel, because you have been strong against God." (Gen. 32:28). "Israel" means literally "a wrestler with God." In the Old Testament a person's name revealed his inner essence. The change of names shows that Jacob's inner nature has been radically changed. This change is the blessing for which Jacob asked. He is no longer Jacob, "a supplanter," but "Israel," a man who has striven with God Himself.

To understand Jacob's strange experience, we must use our imagination to reconstruct what must have been going through his mind that fateful night; he must have roamed back through his storehouse of memories to those dark days of his youth and the deceitful deeds he had perpetrated against his brother and father. He suffered the pain of looking at them from the vantage point of his maturity, and agonized over the egocentric young man he had been. He was struggling with his shadow, the dark one within him. But there was also the matter of Esau and his fate the next day. He was looking death in the face. Tomorrow's dawn might be the last rising sun he would ever see. Before him stretched the Unknown: death, with all of its unanswered questions. Death is one of the great numinous experiences, for when we look at death, which always lies close at hand, we are peering into the totally unknown. What began as a struggle in his mind with his shadow, led to a struggle with the Unknown, and so the whole of the unconscious seized Jacob's ego and wrestled with it. Behind

Jacob's wrestling match is the archetype of totality, what Jung calls the Self or God-image in the soul, a mystery which can be experienced, but never made rational.

After receiving his blessing through his change of name, Jacob asked his Divine Adversary his name, but this was not for Jacob to know. "Why do you ask my name?" the Adversary asked, (Gen. 32:30) and refused to tell him. Moses came to know the name of God, but not Jacob. Great man though he was, Jacob could not have borne this knowledge. To know God's name is to know His inner essence, and this can be frightening and annihilating to the unprepared. Not even Jacob's spiritual courage has prepared him for that kind of an experience. It is literally true, that if a person is suddenly plunged into the Unknown, that unconscious inner realm in which God dwells in the soul, he can become disoriented to the extent of losing his mind. So the Divine Adversary did not give him His name, but left as the sun rose. But first he did a strange thing: he touched Jacob on the thigh, wounding him, so that Jacob went away from that place limping because of his thigh. As Jacob left he gave the place a name—Peniel—which means, "the face of God." Jacob declared, "Because I have seen God face to face, and I have survived." (Gen. 32:31). Then he left Peniel to rejoin his family, limping as he went.

The ease with which the Adversary wounded Jacob makes us suspect that He could have won the struggle at any time against His human antagonist. The meaning of the encounter lay in the struggle itself, and the purpose of the Adversary was to change and test Jacob, not to destroy him. The wound Jacob received is the mark a person carries who encounters spiritual reality as deeply as did Jacob. A person who has an experience of this psychological depth is always wounded by it. It is a way of saying that someone who encounters these things can never go back and be the kind of person he was before. The experience is indelible and changes us forever. It becomes like a wound, constantly reminding us of the spiritual reality we have known, and enforcing upon us a recognition of the finite nature of this little ego of ours in relationship to the awesomeness of God.

Such a spiritual wound is not to be confused with a neurosis or crippling injury. It is not a limiting wound, but a wound through which pours the life of God, a guarantee that after such an experience a person can never again live unaware of spiritual reality. In the cure of souls, we meet with experiences like this. Some people can find what help they need for a certain problem and then return to their former way of life and former state of consciousness. Others are touched deeply in the process by the powers of the unconscious. They are affected so deeply that they will never be the same again. They cannot return to their former selves, but must constantly journey ahead through life, and every day of their lives they are forced to live with the realization that inner reality is but a hair-breadth away. It makes a person a little lonely to be marked by God this way; one is forced to recognize one's difference from others who have not had the experience. But it is also a great blessing, for through such a wounded ego there pours the life of God.

The story of Jacob now moves swiftly to its final scene. Jacob goes on to meet Esau. He must have been a weary man indeed as he went to this encounter with his brother. Unarmed, he goes only with the faith that God will see him through. At first the situation looks grim as Esau approaches with his armed men. Jacob goes up to Esau and bows seven times before his brother. What a different man this Jacob is from the arrogant youth who denied the famished Esau a bowl of soup! And Esau embraces him and weeps. The two brothers hold each other in their arms, their tears giving evidence of their forgiveness of each other and the openness of their hearts. And Jacob declares, "To speak truly, I came into your presence as into the presence of God." (Gen. 33:10).

This happy reconciliation scene suggests that Esau also has gone through a process of psychological development analogous to Jacob's. Unfortunately we know nothing of what has been happening with Esau since the time of his betrayal by Jacob, but his generous attitude and spirit suggest more than simply that his anger has cooled. Perhaps Esau acquired that trait of psychological honesty which had saved his brother from spiritual disaster, and faced up to his own shadow, accepting responsibility for that weakness in himself which had allowed him to give away his birthright for a bowl of soup. Such painful self-confrontation is deeply healing. It is the only way to gain our inner balance and pave the way for our psychological development, and, having faced our own weakness and guilt, we are able to accept and forgive others. We do not know that this is what Esau experienced, but we do know that he is a different person now than the crude and unreflecting person he was as a youth.

So the estranged brothers are reconciled and our story is complete. Jacob has been reconciled to himself, to God, to Esau. Jacob's destiny has been fulfilled.

*   *   *

Epilogue

The spotlight of the Biblical narrative now shifts from Jacob to his son Joseph. Jacob continues to appear now and again in the subsequent story, but is no longer the principal character. We see him mainly as an old man, who has lost his beloved wife, Rachel, and lives with his other wives and his many sons. He is by no means a completely wise person all of the time. No one ever reaches a state of perfection, and Jacob as an old man makes mistakes, just as he did when he was a young man. But his errors are no longer the egocentric faults of his youth, but are the failings of a man who loved deeply, though not always wisely. For while Jacob loved all of his sons and they loved him in turn, he loved Rachel's son Joseph more than the others, and his favoritism showed, and led to disastrous consequences. Jacob continued to display a common failing of his family in the way he lavished affection on one child and discriminated against the others.

There is, however, one other story which points up Jacob's continued spiritual sensitivity and consciousness. Joseph has a dream in which he sees the sun and moon and eleven stars bowing down before him. Naturally Joseph takes it on a personal level, as a sign of his power supremacy over his father, mother, and eleven brothers. Jacob, a wise father at this point, chides him for his arrogance, but he also notes the dream as a portent of a great future for his son and "kept the thing in mind." (Gen. 37:11). He has the wisdom not to feed the young Joseph's conceit, but also the spiritual perception to recognize that perhaps a great destiny is in store for him.

So Jacob lived to be an old man, full of love and anxiety for his children, until at last Joseph brought him and his whole family to the land of Egypt, where Jacob, much loved, died, after bestowing a blessing on each of his sons. Each son received a blessing, but the great blessing went to Joseph. It is interesting to note that Jacob did *not* keep the unthinking tradition which said that the great blessing always went to the eldest son; his great blessing went to Joseph, the one who had obviously been chosen by God For Jacob now knew what was the true birthright of his people: it was the direct relationship between a man and God, the ego and the numinosum, and which man will carry on this relationship is not a matter to be decided by tradition. Then, having performed this last act of consciousness, "he drew his feet up into the bed, and breathing his last was gathered to his people." (Gen. 49:33).

PART TWO

The Slave Who
Ruled A Nation

CHAPTER FOUR

An Arrogant Young Man

There are many parallels between the stories of Jacob and Joseph. This is not surprising since psychological development takes place in certain typical ways. So it will not surprise us to find that Joseph goes through several experiences which are similar to Jacob's.

Like Jacob, Joseph too is an egocentric young man. Joseph does not engage in the sort of shadowy subterfuge and deception practiced by the young Jacob, but, if anything, he is more insufferable. The first report we have shows him to be that universally despised person, a tattle-tale. When Joseph is seventeen we are told that he "informed their father of the evil spoken about them (his brothers)." Joseph's motives for bringing an evil report about his brothers to his father is evidently malicious. He has no reason to want to make his brothers look bad in order to win his father's affection for himself since he is already his father's favorite: "Israel loved Joseph more than all his other sons, for he was the son of his old age." (Gen. 37:2-3).

We do not know as much about the development of Joseph's arrogant egocentricity as we do about Jacob's. In Jacob's case we knew about his mother complex, of Rebekah's favoritism for him, and of her faith that he was destined by God for great things. Rebekah is now dead, and so is Joseph's mother,

47

Rachel. But we do know that Joseph is his father's favorite, and suspect that this favoritism comes, not so much because he was the child of his father's old age, but because he was the child of the much loved Rachel.

Rachel, as we saw in our study of Jacob's life, carried her husband's soul with her, he loved her so intensely. At her death, Jacob may have put on her two children the intense feeling he bore for her. These children may have become like gods to him. One of the images of God is the image of the "Divine Child"; we see him in the Christmas story, and the magic which surrounds the Christ Child. If parents do not have God in the right place, their children can play a god role to them, appearing as magically wonderful beings who can do no wrong. In psychological language we would say that the new life which the parent should be realizing in himself or herself is seen in the child, who then carries a godlike role for the parents. For if we look to other human beings for our source of new life and meaning, they are god to us.

Whenever god is placed upon anyone, that person suffers. No human being can carry god for another human being. If it is another adult who is god for us, sooner or later that relationship will break down, for no person can play the god role indefinitely. If it is a child who carries god for his or her parents, something destructive may take place. Sometimes it is a collision with reality. It is quite a shock for a child who has been raised with the belief that he is next to God to be plunged suddenly into a world which is not at all impressed and couldn't care less.

In Joseph's case, it looks as if the mischief came about because he identified himself with this godlikeness. He believed that he was this wonderfully great person with the divine qualities, and this created in him a "Star" form of egocentricity, a great desire to shine, and receive adulation and homage from others. For Joseph's personality to develop, this destructive egocentricity had to be broken, and we will find as our story progresses that this great Star of a youth suffers the ironic fate of becoming a complete nobody—a slave without even a name to himself. It was strong medicine, but it took this to cure the arrogant Joseph of his inflation and break his unconscious identification with a divine role.

Considering what an arrogant person this tattle-tale brother was, it is not surprising that his brothers came to hate him: "But his brothers, seeing how his father loved him more than all his other sons, came to hate him so much that they could not say a civil word to him." (Gen. 37:4). The hatred of the brothers is all mixed up with their love. They love their father and want his love in return, but they smart under the favoritism Jacob shows to this despised Joseph. Our need for love, when thwarted, easily turns into hatred. It was natural that their jealousy should inspire hatred for Joseph, and that the anger in them should be inflamed by Joseph's extremely irritating personality.

The situation only gets worse when Joseph comes up with two big dreams. In our discussion of Jacob, we noted that the people of the Bible believed in dreams, and Joseph and his brothers are no exception. Tactlessly, Joseph repeats the following dream to his brothers: "Listen," he said, "to this dream I have had. We were binding sheaves in the countryside; and my sheaf, it seemed, rose up and stood upright; then I saw your sheaves gather round and bow to my sheaf." (Gen. 37:6-7). His brothers rightfully take Joseph's telling them the dream as another example of his arrogance. Angrily they exclaim, "'So you want to be king over us, or to lord it over us?' And they hated him still more, on account of his dreams and of what he said." (Gen. 37:8).

The brothers give the dream a Freudian interpretation. Freud said that dreams express, in a disguised fashion, desires which are regarded by the conscious personality as unacceptable for moral or other reasons. The key idea in this theory of dream interpretation is wish fulfillment; our dreams are said to express wishes which we secretly harbor but dare not consciously face. The brothers see Joseph's dream in this light, as the expression of his wish to dominate them, and another example of his conceit.

No doubt the arrogant Joseph had such a wish, though there is no reason to suppose that he repressed his wishes for

moral reasons, but the deeper significance of his dream lies
in its portent of the future. There are dreams in which a person's
destiny is hinted at long before it becomes a reality. Looked
at in this way the dream is a manifestation of the divine destiny
which is at work in Joseph's life. It is an example of the teleological[1] influence which shapes our lives because it draws
us into a future development which is known somewhere in
the unconscious, though it is not yet known to consciousness.

But at this point neither Joseph nor his brothers are conscious enough to take the dream in this way. Joseph just delights
in the inflated view of himself which the dream suggests to
him; he does not realize that, for the dream to be fulfilled,
he must become the kind of person God can use, nor does
he have any inkling that if this dream is to become reality
he must first endure enormous, purifying suffering. Had he
for a moment glimpsed what must come about in his life because
of this dream, he would have been humbled and dismayed,
and would no doubt have kept it to himself. His brothers,
on the other hand, cannot face up to the deeper implications
of the dream. Somewhere in their minds there must have been
the suspicion, "Maybe this is the way it is going to be." But
this objectionable thought was quickly repressed; not allowed
into consciousness, it festered as a disturbing doubt in the unconscious. The seed for the brothers' decision to kill Joseph
is fed by this repressed doubt and fear. When they decide to
murder Joseph it is because they fear him, as well as hate
him.

A wiser young man would have let the matter drop, but
Joseph's hubris knows no bounds. He also suffers from a failing
common to persons with his type of inflation: he supposes no
harm can come to him. As his father's favorite, with his godlike
identification, he feels magically protected against the dangers
which ordinary mortals must fear. So when he has a second

---

[1]Teleological comes from the Greek word telos which means the end
or goal. If something is teleological, it aims toward a goal. In psychology
it means that there is a process of development within us which aims at
a goal which is not known to consciousness but influences us nonetheless
toward a future development.

dream, which, on a superficial level, also suggests his supremacy over his brothers, he flaunts this dream in their faces too: "Look, I have had another dream" he said. "I thought I saw the sun, the moon and eleven stars, bowing to me." (Gen. 37:9-10).

Joseph's arrogance is now so great that even his father scolds him: "A fine dream to have! Are all of us then, myself, your mother[2] and your brothers, to come and bow down to the ground before you?" (Gen. 37:10). But though Jacob wisely chastises Joseph, trying to curb his excessive inflation, he also "kept the thing in mind." Just as Rebekah once saw that a divine destiny was stored up for Jacob, so Jacob now begins to suspect that an unusual destiny may be waiting for Joseph. His brothers, however, hate and fear him all the more.

The fact that Joseph remembered his dreams is a matter of great importance for our understanding of the story. Joseph, even as a youth, was a man who remembered his dreams and paid them careful attention. We hear nothing of his brothers remembering their dreams. Not even his father, Jacob, made a regular habit of remembering his dreams as far as we know, although he was deeply influenced by the few powerful dreams which broke in upon him at crucial times in his life. But Joseph lives so much with his inner world that his brothers call him derisively "the man of dreams."

Joseph's instinctive and lifelong contact with his dreams marks him as a person with an unusual psychology. Time and again the story of Joseph tells us that "Yahweh was with Joseph." No matter how dark and seemingly hopeless his situation later becomes, this refrain, "Yahweh was with Joseph," is repeated. It may be that Yahweh was with him through his dreams; that Joseph's ability to remain in touch with his inner life in this way is what is meant by that repeated refrain. For it is a psychological fact that making friends with one's dreams also makes a friend of the unconscious, and gives us a psychological and spiritual support throughout our lives.

---

[2]According to Gen. 35:19 Joseph's mother, Rachel, is already dead. So we must suppose either that the story refers to another wife of Jacob, or that the story at this point comes from another tradition.

There have been people like Joseph, who live close to their inner worlds, in all cultures. In primitive tribes in Asia and North and South America these people were the shamans, the healers in the community. The shaman, as we noted in our discussion of Jacob's dream of the ladder leading up to heaven, was called to his vocation as seer and healer by a characteristic kind of dream or visionary experience which was accompanied by an acute psychological crisis. Dreams and visions remained an important part of the life of the shaman; he (or she) often received instruction from the spirits in this way, and, through his dreams, maintained a link to heaven. Of course almost all primitive people were oriented to their dreams and took them seriously, but the shaman was generally distinguished by the frequency and vividness of his inner life. He was one of that class of people which William James called the tender minded, in contrast to the tough minded hunter; not that he was psychologically a weaker person, for usually he was a person of extraordinary personality, but he was a person whose consciousness was readily invaded by contents from the unconscious.

Joseph was evidently a person of this type. These people are called to a religious vocation. The root meaning of the word "religious" is thought to come from the Latin word "religare," which means "to bind." The truly religious person is one who is bound to his own inner process. He finds it utterly inescapable and is called upon to serve it. If a person is called upon to be a spokesman for the inner world, he is a healer or prophet and he must obey this calling. If a person was called to be a shaman, for instance, and tried to deny his vocation, he would fall ill and die. A shaman could only stay well by shamanizing.

In our time and culture, unfortunately, we do not recognize such a vocation. The shaman, whose experience was individual, visionary, and healing, has been replaced in religion by the priest or minister, who is called upon to be the exponent of a collectivized tradition and doctrine. The doctor is now a man of science, and no longer functions professionally in the role of the charismatic healer. The signs that someone is called upon to this inner vocation as a healer are readily confused with symptoms of severe neurosis or even psychosis—indeed, that is what they become if the vocation is denied—so some people who might actually be called to a religious, shamanic vocation become ill because they do not understand the true nature of what appears, from the outside, to be only an illness.

Joseph's two dreams, which his brothers took only as wish fulfillment, can be understood as his call to serve the inner world. Psychologically they show the ego and the Self, or God image within the soul, in creative juxtaposition. Of course Joseph is not yet the kind of psychologically developed person these two dreams depict. Some dreams show actual situations, others describe possibilities. These dreams are saying "such a psychological development is possible in this person." But Joseph had a long way to go in his development before this possibility of greatness could be realized in him. At this point he has merely identified with godlikeness and has become unbearably inflated. His egocentricity and conceit must first be purged away through great suffering before he can fulfill the destiny foretold by his dreams. Like a true shaman, he must first be psychologically dismembered and die, and then be restored, before he is ready for his spiritual vocation. The rest of our story will be taken up largely with this transformation in Joseph.

CHAPTER FIVE

Into The Depths

After Joseph tells his brothers his two dreams, they are sent out into the wilderness by their father to care for the flocks and herds, but Joseph, because he is his father's favorite, stays at home. Later Jacob is anxious to know how things are going with the brothers, and sends Joseph to find them and bring back a report. Joseph is happy to go. Perhaps he thinks this is another chance to bring back to his father a bad report about his brothers. His naive readiness to go shows how unconscious he is; he is totally unaware that he is putting himself in any danger.

While looking for his brothers in the countryside, Joseph comes across a stranger, who asks him, "What are you looking for?" The question is fateful. Joseph should be looking for the meaning of his dreams, but he does not yet understand any of this. He replies, "I am looking for my brothers. Please tell me where they are pasturing their flock." (Gen. 37:15-16). It is because he is not searching for the right thing that he gets into trouble.

In the Bible when an unknown man appears like this he can be taken as an angel; very often angels, that is messengers from God, appeared so much like human beings that they were mistaken for men. An example of this is found, for instance, in Abraham's dialogue with the three angels of Yahweh, whom at first he took for ordinary men and welcomed into his house. (Gen. 18:1-15). Joseph's unawareness of the identity of the man, and his lack of insight into the meaning of the fateful question, show that he is not yet prepared to undertake the divine calling which his dreams have foreshown. If this man was an angel and Joseph had entered into a discussion with him, perhaps the catastrophic events soon to follow could have been avoided.

When something is to come through to us from within, the Spirit tries every means it can to help us get the message. But if we miss the message, that is, if we fail to recognize and speak with the angel, it is often left to outer events to force us into greater awareness. Suppose, for instance, we are on a collision course with our own truth and reality; that our conscious attitude is wrong, and we are being confronted from within by the unconscious which opposes it. The situation is ripe for an accident. If we can listen to the inner voice, and come to terms with the opposing force within us which wants to cut us off from the false direction we are taking, it will be much easier than having it happen to us on the outside in the form, perhaps, of an acute accident, or some other catastrophe. But Joseph is too unconscious and egocentric to be ready for such a dialogue and so the man simply answers, "They have moved on from here; indeed I heard them say, 'Let us go to Dothan'." (Gen. 37:17).

Joseph follows the stranger's directions and finds his brothers. They see him coming in the distance and begin at once to plot against him. The naive young Joseph is apparently unaware of danger from the intense hatred he has aroused in his brothers. He fancies himself still in the charmed circle of his father's affection, and, with his godlike opinion of himself, walks blindly into the jaws of disaster. The brothers, of course, have long been consumed with hate-filled fantasies of destroying Joseph, and are delighted to see him walking into their hands. Scornfully they declare, "Here comes the man of dreams. Come on, let us kill him and throw him into some well; we can say that a wild beast devoured him. Then we shall see what

becomes of his dreams." (Gen. 37:19-20). The last phrase suggests again their fear of Joseph; that his dreams might, after
all, have a ring of truth.

Fortunately, one of the brothers is moved by another sen-
timent. Reuben, the first-born son of Leah, sees the terrible
nature of the deed his brothers are contemplating. He recognizes
that in their present state of mind there is no possibility of
persuading them not to take revenge on Joseph, so he proposes
that instead of killing him at once they throw him into a nearby
dry well, hoping this will give him time to devise a plan for
freeing Joseph later. The brothers agree, and when Joseph arrives
he is roughly seized, stripped of the hated coat of many colors[1]
which his father had made for him, and thrown into the empty
hole.

While the brothers are eating, no doubt making merry
while Joseph, terrified, pleads for mercy, a group of Ishmaelite
traders come along on their way to Egypt. Judah suddenly
has an idea. "What do we gain by killing our brother and
covering up his blood?" he reasons. "Come, let us sell him
to the Ishmaelites, but let us not do any harm to him. After
all, he is our brother, and our own flesh." (Gen. 37:26-27).

Judah's plan is accepted, but not because of any sympathy
for Joseph or feeling of compassion because he is their brother.
It was not compassion, but fear of the consequences of shedding
the blood of a kinsman which caused them to change their
mind, for it was thought in that day that the blood of a murdered
man cried out from the ground for vengeance. That is why
Judah spoke of "covering up his blood." The blood of a murdered man must be buried so heaven would not discover the
crime and take vengeance. Besides, in this way they would
receive money for Joseph, and having him as a slave in Egypt
was as good as killing him anyway. No one expected slaves
in Egypt to live for very long.

So Joseph is sold to the Ishmaelites as a slave. Reuben
was not there when all this took place, and when he returns
and finds Joseph gone he is distraught. "What am I going

---

[1]Or long sleeved coat, the preferred, but less poetic wording of modern
translators.

to do?" he cries out in anguish. Perhaps Reuben was trying to spare his father the pain of losing Joseph. The other brothers also have their father to worry about. What will they tell him? How will they explain Joseph's disappearance? A lie must be invented to cover up their evil deed, and so it is decided to take Joseph's coat, dip it in the blood of a slain goat, and show it to their father to make him believe that Joseph was apparently killed by a wild animal. Jacob is agonized when he is shown the blood-soaked coat of his favorite son. He tears his clothes, puts on sackcloth, and goes into extended mourning for him. The sons try to comfort their father; after all, they do love him, and his anguish arouses the furies of guilt in their minds. But he refuses to be consoled, declaring, "No, I will go down in mourning to Sheol, beside my son." (Gen. 37:35).

The brothers are now bearing a heavy burden of guilt, which works upon them during the years which elapse between the time of Joseph's disappearance into Egypt, and the time when they are reunited with him at the end of our story. They could push their guilt into the unconscious, but it could not be resolved. It formed a complex within them which surfaced later in their lives and, as we shall see, became the focal point many years later for their own psychological development.

There is a gap in the Biblical account between the time Joseph is sold to the Ishmaelites and when he appears as a slave in Egypt. There is also a marked contrast between the arrogant young man who provoked his brothers to their awful deed, and the responsible and humble young man whom we meet in Egypt. Evidently Joseph's experience was enormously transforming for him. We will have to reconstruct what he went through with our imagination to understand this transformation.

When Joseph first arrived at his brothers' camp he felt secure as his father's favorite. Then he was suddenly seized, stripped of his garments, and cast into the pit. Here he must have trembled with fear while he heard his brothers laughing at him and plotting his death. He pleaded for mercy, but his pleas were ignored. He could hardly have been relieved when Judah proposed his plan to sell him as a slave to Egypt instead of murdering him outright, for Pharaoh was involved in massive building projects, involving thousands of slaves who worked under unbearable conditions pulling gigantic blocks of stone into place in the blazing desert sun. These slaves could not have lasted more than a few years, and their lot was so terrible that they must have often longed for the death which awaited them. So when Joseph was placed in chains and carried with the traders far away from home, never (in his mind) to see his father again, facing only torture and agonizing labor, it was like a death experience. On that ghastly journey to Egypt the young Joseph died. His godlike pretensions were utterly destroyed, his Star form of egocentricity reached point zero, and vanished.

Joseph's journey to Egypt was analogous to Jacob's exile into the wilderness, and as we shall see, to Moses' flight to Midian. For persons who are called upon for a great inner development and awareness of God, such a "night sea journey," an experience of ego-shattering depression and despair, is typical. The experience of Jacob, Joseph, and Moses is similar because it is archetypal. To be sure, had they been less fixed in their egocentricity, their experiences might have been less frightful. Perhaps others of us need only experience a mild depression or difficult anxiety, not such a totally annihilating experience as Joseph had to undergo. But for Joseph it was a necessity. His egocentricity was so great that it took a medicine this strong to cure him.

Of course this medicine could also have killed him. Had Joseph persisted in his egocentricity, allowed himself to languish in self-pity or despair, abandoned God or sought suicide, his frightful journey would have been a poison rather than a medicine. This is the way it is when we are confronted by what can be called the dark side of God: it can be a poison which destroys us, or a medicine which cures us. Which it will be depends on how we respond to it. Joseph evidently responded to it in a creative way. He must have seen, on that lonely journey into slavery, what a conceited ass he had been, and how his arrogance had brought this upon himself.

After many days of travel, the traders arrived with Joseph in Egypt and the young man was brought to the auction block for sale. A healthy young male like this would ordinarily have become a slave-laborer, his imminent death a certainty. But at what must have seemed like the last moment, Joseph was snatched from death as a slave on one of Pharaoh's back-breaking projects. A certain captain in Pharaoh's army named Potiphar went to the slave market the day Joseph was to be sold. Something in Joseph's bearing, perhaps the intelligence which obviously the young man possessed, impressed Potiphar. He decided to buy Joseph himself to help him run his household. It was rare, but a few of the most intelligent and promising slaves were used in this way by wealthy people. Their lot was relatively fortunate. Though they remained slaves throughout their lives, they could live a comfortable existence; life was possible for them.

So Joseph is taken into Potiphar's household, and proves himself such a capable person that very soon he is placed in charge of the whole household. Here we can see that Joseph's egocentricity is gone. His arrogance has been burned away on the journey to Egypt, and the young Joseph is deeply grateful for the positive turn in his fortunes which sent him to Potiphar. Joseph expresses his gratitude to Potiphar by doing as good a job as possible, and Joseph proves to be a man of remarkable abilities which his master soon comes to appreciate and reward.

Our story tells us, "Yahweh was with Joseph, and everything went well with him ... and when his master saw how Yahweh was with him and how Yahweh made everything succeed that he turned his hand to, he was pleased with Joseph and made him his personal attendant ... So he left Joseph to handle all his possessions." (Gen. 39:2-6). I have already suggested that "Yahweh was with Joseph" means that he was receiving positive support from the unconscious and helpful guidance from his dreams. This comes about when consciousness has the right attitude. We receive back from our inner world a reflection of the face we turn toward it. Had Joseph remained caught in his egocentricity, or had he fallen into sullenness or self-pity, the inner face of the unconscious would have been hostile to him, and Yahweh could not have been with him. But Joseph's attitude is correct, and so he receives great support from within.

But just as Joseph's fortunes begin to improve, a new catastrophe develops, more grim than when his brothers sold him as a slave. The first time, Joseph was to blame for his plight; this time he does not deserve what happened to him. This part of the story begins with a rare bit of physical description:[2] "Now Joseph was well built and handsome, and it happened some time later that his master's wife looked desirously at him and said, 'Sleep with me.'" (Gen. 39:7-8).

Joseph must have been an impressive figure, combining a powerful physique and handsome features with a general bearing of great intelligence and forcefulness. As for Potiphar's wife, who has developed a desire for him, perhaps she was lonely. As an officer in the army, her husband was no doubt away a great deal. Maybe their relationship was also deficient or broken, and perhaps her life was without love. At any rate, she conceives a desire for Joseph and tries to seduce him, and if she felt disloyal because she was breaking her relationship with Potiphar, she does not let it stop her.

If Joseph had accepted her offer to make love, it would have been hard to find fault with him. After all, what did he, as a slave, owe to his master? *He* was being exploited, so why should he not exploit Potiphar? Besides, as the lover of Potiphar's wife he stood to gain all kinds of favors from her, but if he rejected her he might create a dangerous enemy. But Joseph does reject her seductive offer, on the basis of his loyalty to Potiphar: "Because of me, my master does not concern himself with what happens in the house; he has handed over all his possessions to me. He is no more master in this house than I am. He has withheld nothing from me except yourself, because you are his wife. How could I do anything so wicked, and sin against God?" Potiphar's wife is persistent, but Joseph is not dissuaded: "Although she spoke to Joseph day after day he would not agree to sleep with her and surrender to her." (Gen. 39:8-10).

In following the life of Jacob, we saw how he developed

---

[2]Only occasionally does the Bible offer us any physical description of people. We have a brief description of the young David, and of Saul in 1 Samuel, but these are rare exceptions.

his capacity for eros and relationship through his love for Rachel. Jacob became a deeply related man who cared about other people and won their love in return. Now we see the same thing with Joseph. He rejects Potiphar's wife because of his relationship with Potiphar. For Joseph, sexual union with Potiphar's wife would have been a loveless embrace. There would have been physical fulfillment, but no eros. To be true to the principle of eros, the great feminine principle of relatedness, Joseph remains loyal to his master, who has trusted him.

The development of capacity for relationship is a sign of great personality development, but especially in a man, for whom the relationship side of life often comes less naturally than for a woman. So undeveloped is eros in many men that they mistake sexuality for relationship. Joseph is more developed than this. For him the principle of relationship is one of the highest principles; to offend it is to sin against God Himself. This is the basis on which Joseph refuses the offer of Potiphar's wife, rather than an outer moral commandment or injunction. It shows that Joseph follows his inner truth, that his moral conduct is rooted in his own psychological development. He relates to his God within and obeys the ethic of creativity.

Unfortunately for Joseph, there is truth to the statement, "Hell hath no fury like a woman scorned."[3] Potiphar's wife is not at all interested in the nobility of Joseph's motives for declining her offer to make love. She only experiences it as a humiliating rejection, and wants to destroy Joseph to gain her revenge. This shows us that she did not love Joseph, but only desired him. One day, when no one else was around except Joseph, Potiphar's wife asked Joseph once more to sleep with her. Joseph refused again, and she became so violent that he fled, but not before she had wrenched his outer garment away from him. When Potiphar returned, his wife said, "The Hebrew slave you brought us came to insult me. But when I screamed and called out he left his garment by my side and made his escape." (Gen. 39:17-18).

Potiphar is angry and indignant. Without asking Joseph

---

[3]William Congreve (1670–1729) from "The Mourning Bride." Act III, Sc. 8.

for his side of the story, he sends for his soldiers. Joseph is seized, and, with no chance to defend himself, is banished to one of Pharaoh's dungeons. Clearly Potiphar's capacity for relatedness is far less developed than Joseph's. He has no thought of Joseph's loyalty to him, or the beginnings of a friendship with his helpful slave, but thinks only of the supposed insult given to him. Perhaps the master-slave relationship asserted itself. To have consulted with Joseph and asked him his side of the story would have been to treat Joseph as a person in his own right; as a slave, Joseph was less than a person in Potiphar's eyes. Not so with Joseph. He had transcended the master-slave relationship with Potiphar, and regarded him as a person whose trust he did not wish to betray.

Once again Joseph's fortunes are at the nadir. What has happened to him now is worse than his previous experience. When he was first sold as a slave, there was at least some hope that he might wind up in a good position, as did indeed happen. But in Pharaoh's dungeon his situation is well nigh hopeless. Being a slave, he has no rights; he cannot expect a trial, the most he can hope for is that he will be forgotten, for if he is remembered his fate will surely be execution. But to be forgotten meant to live forever in the dark horror of Pharaoh's prison, and this time he did not deserve his fate. Earlier he could at least realize that he had brought his fate upon himself by his arrogant attitude, but this time he had acted out of the best in himself.

Under such circumstances it would not have been surprising if Joseph had abandoned his faith and rejected his relationship with Yahweh. Who could have judged him if this had happened? And no doubt it did happen this way for a time, but it did not remain this way; instead we are told, surprisingly, that "Yahweh was with Joseph." Then, remarkably enough, we learn that in a short time Joseph's ability and integrity had been recognized by the warden of the dungeon and he rose to a position of some authority, working as the warden's administrative assistant. As for Potiphar, he forgot Joseph completely, which, under the circumstances, was just as well.

There were several qualities Joseph had developed which enabled him to rise above his depressing circumstances. One was his custom of making the best of everything. Some people feel that they are above lowly things in life, and if life forces them to a subordinate position they feel humiliated. Their lowly status is such a threat to their egocentricity that they can only defend themselves by refusing to work hard at the task which life has given them. "I am above that," they say in haughty disdain, or, in an equally egocentric way, "Oh I'm not worth it." But Joseph gave himself wholeheartedly to every task which came his way. When a slave in Potiphar's household, he gave it the best he had; now a prisoner in a dungeon, he still tried to accomplish the most he could. With such an attitude, circumstances improve. When we do the best job possible in our present situation, no matter how lowly or dreadful it is, life has a way of bringing a better one to us.

Secondly, it was fortunate for Joseph that he was a realistic man, not an idealist. An idealist would have been so disillusioned at the negative turn of events that the other side of his idealism would have come up—cynicism. The idealist and the cynic are a pair of opposites: turn one over and you get the other. If Joseph had been such a man, that would have been the end of him, and certainly the end of his faith in God. But Joseph did not expect God to be the guarantor that goodness would prevail, nor did he see his relationship with God as some kind of bargain in which God would protect him from evil in return for his faithful worship. If this had been the case, he would certainly have succumbed to the "Why did God let this happen to me?" attitude which is characteristic of so many of us whose religious attitude has not matured. But Joseph did not see God as a guarantor of goodness and protection, but as a source of guidance in the midst of whatever circumstances life might bring.

Perhaps because of his healthy religious attitude, Joseph did not languish in that last resort of our egocentricity; self-pity. Nothing would have been easier for Joseph than to have wallowed in feelings of being sorry for himself. "What have I done to deserve this? How life has picked on me! How God has failed me!" Perhaps at first this is how he felt, but eventually Joseph hung on to his own inner Center, and, no doubt, watched for signs of hope in his dreams.

For there is a psychological Center within us, a point where our personalities become connected to God. If we can relate to this inner Center, we find ourselves enclosed in a psychologically and spiritually protective and strengthening circle, and our inner integrity is preserved even in the midst of extreme adversity. Joseph had found this Center. When his egocentricity was burned away on the journey to Egypt, he found his Center and began to live from it. In all things he looked for the Will of Heaven, and sought to bring his actions and his attitudes into accordance with it. He continued to follow his dreams, and looked there for Yahweh's guidance, and, since we are told "Yahweh was with him," we can assume that his dreams were helpful to him. He must also have resorted to that creative form of prayer which does not seek to manipulate life, but tries to relate the ego to the Center. All of this gave Joseph strength. He did not disintegrate in Pharaoh's dungeon; he did not become bitter, cynical or self-pitying. With this attitude it was only a matter of time until he became as free on the outside as he was on the inside.

CHAPTER SIX

The Turning Point

It was Joseph's ability to interpret dreams which brought the turning point in his fortunes. Two of Pharaoh's former officials, his chief cup-bearer and his chief baker, are thrown into the dungeon with Joseph. One day Joseph observes that they are in a depression. "Why these black looks today?" he asks them. (Gen. 40:7). It is interesting that Joseph was concerned about their welfare. The incident hints that Joseph had something of the healer in him, a quality which goes along with the shamanistic type of personality we described earlier.

It is, by the way, a rare thing in the Old Testament, in which the healer is almost totally absent. The prophets of the Old Testament are primarily persons who proclaim the word of Yahweh relative to social, political, or religious situations, and not shamanistic healers. The ancient Hebrews were one of the few primitive peoples without healers who played a significant role in their community. Perhaps this was due to the lack of the feminine element in the image of God. Yahweh is a predominantly masculine deity, and healing does not take place without the feminine element. In the New Testament, the feminine element re-enters through Mary, the mother of Jesus, whom the Church later called "Theotokos," the bearer of God. So here we have an emphasis on healing which is missing in the Old Testament.[1] However, as we noted, Joseph is close to his feminine side. His interest in the welfare of the cup-bearer and baker is part of the same differentiated capacity for relationship which caused him to be loyal to Potiphar. This time it has different results, and leads ultimately to his release from prison.

The cup-bearer and the baker explain to Joseph that they have each had a dream, but are downcast because there is no one to interpret them. Dreams were regarded as important in ancient Egypt, as well as in Babylonia and with the ancient Hebrews, and the cup-bearer and the baker hope for guidance from their dreams which will help them in their present crisis. Naturally they are upset, since they have had the dreams, but cannot find anyone to help them understand them. But dreams, of course, are right up Joseph's alley. "Are not interpretations God's business?" he asks. "Come, tell me." (Gen. 40:8).

Nothing could be farther from the mind of a typical priest or minister of our day than the thought that the interpretation of dreams is God's business, and therefore is the concern of His commissioned ministers. As a result, many of us are still shut up in a psychological prison, unable to move out because we cannot comprehend the Word of God. Being in a prison can come about in many ways. We do not need a physical dungeon, for we can be shut up in the dungeon of our own egos, walled in by our materialism, rationalism, and egocentricity. Some of the young people today seem to be trying to blast out of their psychic prisons by the use of drugs. That is a symptom of our loss of contact with our own souls, a loss which is partly the result of our failure today to understand dreams.

The cup-bearer and the baker are delighted to learn that Joseph has skill in such matters, and the butler ventures his dream first. "In my dream," he relates, "I saw a vine in front

---

[1]We do, of course, have a few stories of healing in the Old Testament. Elijah, for instance, restores the widow's son to life (1 Kings 17:17-24) and Elisha heals Naaman the Syrian (2 Kings 5:1-27). But these are rare exceptions. See the fine treatment in Morton Kelsey's book, *Healing and Christianity*, Harper and Row, 1973.

of me. On the vine were three branches; no sooner had it budded than it blossomed, and its clusters became ripe grapes. I had Pharaoh's cup in my hand; I picked the grapes and squeezed them into Pharaoh's cup, and put the cup into Pharaoh's hand." (Gen. 40:9-11).

Joseph was no doubt happy that he could give the cupbearer a favorable interpretation: in three days, he told the anxious cup-bearer, he would be released from prison and restored to his place in Pharaoh's court. In return for his help with the dream Joseph only asks that he remember him when he is released, and speak favorably to Pharaoh about his situation.

The baker, who has been listening carefully to what Joseph told the cup-bearer, and has heard the favorable answer, now ventures to tell his dream. "I too had a dream," he says; "there were three trays of cakes on my head. In the top tray there were all kinds of Pharaoh's favourite cakes, but the birds ate them off the tray on my head." (Gen. 40:16-17). But alas for the baker, Joseph is compelled to interpret his dream unfavorably. In three days, he tells him, Pharaoh will hang him, and the birds will eat the flesh off his bones.

It may seem just chance that the cup-bearer's dream was favorable and the baker's dream unfavorable, but the key to this lies in the different attitudes the two had to the unconscious. Notice that the butler was willing to risk himself with his dream, not knowing what the interpretation would be, while the baker waited until he felt reassured that the outcome would favor him; he was only willing to risk himself with the unconscious if it would suit his purposes. Because he had the wrong attitude toward things of the Spirit, the unconscious had turned against him, as was indicated by his dream.

One would think that the cup-bearer would have been so grateful to Joseph that he would, immediately upon his release from the prison, have pled his case before Pharaoh, but as soon as he was freed from the dungeon, and life once more looked good to him, he forgot all about his benefactor. When we are ill, in desperate straits, or in some kind of crisis, we are often open to receiving help and a new attitude, but when life resumes its ordinary rounds, there is a tendency in us to want to forget the previous unpleasantness. I can think of examples, for instance, in which people who were depressed or anxious turned to their dreams and inner life for help and received it. But as soon as they were well they forgot all about the unconscious and its message for them, and, as a result, soon became ill again. So the cup-bearer forgot about Joseph, while the baker, of course, was executed, and Joseph continued to languish in prison.

Then, two years after the butler rejoined Pharaoh's court, Pharaoh himself had a powerful dream. In his dream he "was standing by the Nile, and there, coming up from the Nile, were seven cows, sleek and fat, and they began to feed among the rushes. And seven other cows, ugly and lean, came up from the Nile after them; and these went over and stood beside the other cows on the bank of the Nile. The ugly and lean cows ate the seven sleek and fat cows." Pharaoh awoke, noted the dream, then fell asleep again and dreamed a second time: "There, growing on one stalk, were seven ears of corn full and ripe. And sprouting up after them came seven ears of corn, meagre and scorched by the east wind. The scanty ears of corn swallowed the seven full and ripe ears of corn." (Gen. 41:1-7). Then Pharaoh awakened, full of concern and anxiety over these two powerful night experiences.

The two dreams are almost identical. Such repeated dreams are always particularly important to understand. It is as though the unconscious is insisting on some special point or message. Pharaoh realized that something unusually important was being said to him in these dreams, and called in his magicians and wise men to interpret them, but they could offer him no help. Then the cup-bearer remembered Joseph. "Today," he said to Pharaoh, "I must recall my offenses. Pharaoh was angry with his servants and put myself and the chief baker under arrest in the house of the commander of the guard. We had a dream on the same night, he and I, and each man's dream had a meaning for himself. There was a young Hebrew with us, one of the slaves belonging to the commander of the guard. We told our dreams to him and he interpreted them, giving each of us the interpretation of his dream. It turned out just as he interpreted for us: I was restored to my place, but the other man was hanged." (Gen. 41:9-13).

So Pharaoh sends for Joseph. We can imagine how surprised Joseph must have been, two years after the cup-bearer had left the prison, to be mysteriously summoned from the dungeon, no doubt washed and shaved, given a fresh change of clothes, and presented before Pharaoh. Pharaoh then tells his dreams to the Hebrew slave. No one else had been able to understand the dreams, but Joseph confidently replies, "I do not count. It is God who will give Pharaoh a favourable answer." (Gen. 41:16).

We can see what a long way Joseph has come from the arrogant egocentricity of his youth. His need to be the Star is gone; he does not need to claim glory for himself, but gives it to God. He is only the instrument to be used by the Greater Wisdom within him. It took a terrible journey to Egypt and enormous suffering to bring this about, but the bitter medicine had its effect, and Joseph is at last ready for his great life work.

Joseph proceeds to the interpretation. He sees immediately that both dreams are giving the same message, so it must be important, and must have to do with events to come. Joseph takes them as warning dreams, portents of the future, such as might occur to a ruler who was responsible for the welfare of his people (whereas the dreams of the cup-bearer and baker concern only themselves). Seven years of plenty will come, Joseph tells Pharaoh, symbolized in the dreams by the seven fat cows and the seven rich ears of corn, but then will come seven years of terrible famine and the fruits of the years of plenty will be eaten up. "The famine that is to follow," he says, "will be so very severe that no one will remember what plenty the country enjoyed. The reason why the dream came to Pharaoh twice is because the event is already determined by God, and God is impatient to bring it about." (Gen. 41:31-32).

Then Joseph does something surprising: he comes up with a master plan to avoid the impending catastrophe. "Pharaoh," he says, "should now choose a man who is intelligent and wise to govern the land of Egypt. Pharaoh should take action

and appoint supervisors over the land, and impose a tax of
one-fifth on the land of Egypt during the seven years of plenty.
They will collect all food produced during these good years
that are coming. They will store the corn in Pharaoh's name,
and place the food in the towns and hold it there. This food
will serve as a reserve for the land during the seven years
of famine that will afflict the land of Egypt. And so the land
will not be destroyed by the famine." (Gen. 41:33-36).

This is a startling example of Joseph's uncanny combination
of psychic power with worldly wisdom and practical administrative capacity. Joseph is becoming a whole person. His introverted side, which enables him to peer into the world of
dreams, and his extraverted side, which gives him a feeling
for the practical needs of the situation, are working together
beautifully. His great intelligence with regard to things of the
Spirit is matched by his shrewd practicality. He is as good
a businessman and man of the world as his father, Jacob, and
far more developed than Jacob as a seer. What made Joseph
so truly great is this enormous development of his personality
in all directions, a feat rarely accomplished, for most of us
make a one-sided identification with a certain aspect of ourselves
and neglect other psychological functions and attitudes.

Joseph's wholeness evidently impressed Pharaoh too, for
on the spot he is made the Chancellor or Prime Minister of
Egypt, and is entrusted with the vastly important task of organizing the realm for the fourteen crucial years to come. Pharaoh asks his ministers, "Can we find any other man like this,
possessing the spirit of God?" Then he says to Joseph, "Seeing
that God has given you knowledge of all this, there can be
no one as intelligent and wise as you. You shall be my chancellor,
and all my people shall respect your orders; only this throne
shall set me above you." (Gen. 41:38-40).

So Joseph is publicly proclaimed in Egypt as the Pharaoh's
Prime Minister, is given authority second only to Pharaoh himself, and is married to the daughter of the most important
priest in the land of Egypt. We are told that he was thirty
years old at the time, so he was still a young man. He promptly
set to work and went throughout the land organizing and ad-
ministering a vast food conservation program. During the seven

years of plenty "Joseph stored the corn like the sand of the sea, so much that they stopped reckoning, since it was beyond all estimating." (Gen. 41:49).

Joseph has come a long way since the time he was sold as a slave to the Ishmaelite traders. But it is not chance that has led him at last to his high position. The outer circumstances of a person's life are inextricably bound up with the inner circumstances. Had Joseph remained caught in his arrogant, youthful inflation, he would certainly have been destroyed long ago. Had he given up and ceased to follow the Voice of God through his dreams, his life might also have come to nothing. But Joseph succeeded in that most difficult, important spiritual task; keeping a relationship with his inner Center, while at the same time remaining aware that his was a mortal limited human existence. In this way he acquired that combination of humbleness and enlarged personality development which leads to true greatness. Joseph was a king in the dungeon long before he became a ruler of men in Pharaoh's Egypt. First he ruled himself; then he was ready to rule men.

CHAPTER SEVEN

Joseph's Brothers

The remainder of our story focuses on Joseph's brothers. When we studied the story of Jacob, we found reason to believe that Esau, as well as Jacob, had undergone a process of psychological development, which, though it was not as extensive as Jacob's, was still sufficient to be the basis for the reconciliation of the two brothers. Now we will see that the same thing happens with Joseph's brothers.

Certain individuals are called upon to achieve a greatly accentuated consciousness and highly developed personality. History eventually recognizes many of these figures as spiritual giants among us. The history of the Bible centers around the lives and insights of a number of these highly gifted individuals whose own conscious development lifted the consciousness of a whole people. Not all of us can achieve the psychological and spiritual development of a Jacob, Joseph, or Moses, but each of us in our way, according to our own individual gifts and calling, is summoned to achieve a measure of psychological awareness and personal integration. Jesus seemed to be saying this when he said, "For many are called, but few are chosen." (Matt. 22:14).

Perhaps one reason why many Christians have failed to hear the words of Jesus in this way is that our expectation of salvation is too passive. Christ has done it all for us, we are told, and all we need to do is to believe, since we are utterly helpless to do anything ourselves. We are taught to look to the Cross as our only hope, forgetting that Jesus himself said, "If anyone wants to be a follower of mine, let him renounce himself and take up his cross every day and follow me." (Luke 9:23).

Joseph Campbell, in his highly readable book *Myths to Live By,* speaks of the kitten people and the monkey people, an idea which comes out of India. The kitten, when lost or in need, cries out "meow, meow," and its mother comes and carries it to safety. But when a band of monkeys is streaking through the forest the baby monkeys can be seen hanging on to their mothers for dear life; whether they make it or not is up to them. There are times when we must be kitten people, and fall back utterly upon God and His action for our help, but there are other times when we ourselves must make the effort. Then it does no good to point to Jesus as "the Man" and adulate him and glorify him, if this means that we overlook the call from God to look to ourselves, and take up the Cross as our own path to growth and consciousness.

The story of Joseph's brothers brings no comfort to those who would like to project onto Jesus the task of becoming a conscious and developed person. They cannot escape from their own call to spiritual and psychological growth by revolving around Jesus like serfs to a master in what Fritz Kunkel used to call a "feudal relationship." For Joseph's brothers, each in his own way and according to his own ability, also undergo a process of psychological development. They do not reach the differentiation of personality which Joseph achieves, but they do suffer through their own process and arrive at their own development. In Joseph's brothers we can see ourselves, and know that even if we cannot be a Joseph, we can be one of his brethren.

Their story resumes when the famine spreads to the land of Canaan. Faced with starvation, Jacob hears there is grain for sale in Egypt, and he sends his sons to buy food so they will not starve. Only Benjamin, the youngest, and, like Joseph, the son of the beloved Rachel, remains at home. The sons make the journey to Egypt and present themselves before Joseph to petition for permission to buy food. Of course they do not recognize this Prime Minister of Egypt as their brother, but Joseph recognizes them. He does not reveal himself to them, however, but speaks to them harshly as though they were strangers to him. As the brothers bow down before him, Joseph remembers the dreams of his youth in which the sheaves of his brothers bowed before his, and the sun, moon, and eleven stars bowed before him. This recollection of his boyhood dreams gives him perspective on his present situation. An ordinary man would have indulged himself in vengeance, now that his enemies were within his power, but Joseph now understands that his dreams were a call from God to a high destiny. If he uses this great power God has given him for vindictive purposes, it will be a sin against the God Who has always been with him, and it will ultimately destroy him.

So he decides to test the brothers. Even though they tell him where they are from, of their father, and of Benjamin who remains at home, they are accused of being spies, and are kept in prison for three days. Then on the third day Joseph tells them if they wish to prove their story to him they must leave one of their number as a hostage, return home, and bring back the youngest brother, Benjamin. The brothers are dismayed, for they know that Benjamin is their father's heart and soul, and his main reason for living. Now they remember their sin against Joseph, and miserably they cry out to each other, "Truly we are being called to account for our brother. We saw his misery of soul when he begged our mercy, but we did not listen to him, and now this misery has come home to us." Reuben, who tried to help Joseph, adds, "Did I not tell you not to wrong the boy? But you did not listen, and now we are brought to account for his blood." (Gen. 42:21-22).

All this was spoken in Joseph's presence, and he, of course, understood everything they said, though the brothers did not realize it. He realizes his brothers' regret over their action against him, and, deeply moved, he begins to weep so bitterly that he is forced to leave their presence.

Here is the guilt complex of Joseph's brothers. When they threw Joseph into the pit, sold him as a slave, and rejected his pleas for mercy, they repressed their guilt. Consumed with their hatred of him, they rationalized their actions, and buried the voice of conscience deep in their hearts (the heart is the Biblical synonym for what we call the unconscious). But nothing is ever forgotten by the unconscious, and things do not cease to exist simply because they have been repressed. The brothers' guilt gnawed at them from within for many years, no doubt continually fed by the anguish of their father, who would not be consoled over the loss of Joseph. It was essential, if the healing and growth of the brothers was to take place, that their guilt come to the surface of consciousness where it could be suffered, faced, and integrated.

It is helpful to distinguish between guilt feelings and real guilt. Guilt feelings come from a more or less distorted conscience made up of the collective attitudes of other people—parents, educators, religious leaders—which have been taken into oneself and which act as a kind of collectivized voice. Often our psychological development requires that false guilt feelings be overcome, that we become free of the tyranny of collectivized attitudes within us. But in addition to this, there is such a thing as true guilt. When we sin against the truth of our own nature, against the very order of life, then we *are* guilty. We then do not just feel guilty, or seem guilty, we are guilty.

If we allow false guilt feelings to possess us, it is a crippling thing, but the only way to deal with real guilt is to take it upon ourselves consciously as a psychological burden to carry. If real guilt is repressed, it will fester and poison us, as it did Joseph's brothers. The cure lies in taking a responsible attitude toward our real guilt: "Yes, what I did was a sin against God and life and I now assume proper responsibility for it." When we have such an attitude, we feel pain, but it is not a neurotic, sickening pain. Real guilt, repressed, makes us sick; when faced, it can lead to the healing of the soul.

In spite of their anguish, the brothers have no alternative except to leave Simeon as a hostage, and return home to implore their father to let them bring Benjamin back to Egypt. So they prepare for the return journey, but Joseph secretly gave an order to fill each man's sack with corn, give them provisions for the journey, and replace each of the brother's money. Their anxiety was almost more than they could bear when they camped on the way home, opened their sacks, and discovered their money in each one. "Their hearts sank, and they looked at one another in panic, saying, 'What is this that God has done to us?'" (Gen. 42:28).

We saw what a profoundly painful but transforming experience it was for Joseph when he was sold as a slave, and how his journey to Egypt was his "night sea journey" of darkness and despair. Something like this now occurs with Joseph's brothers. Their painful journey back to Canaan, their panic when they discover the money in their sacks, and the distress they go through when they tell their father they must take Benjamin back with them, is their night sea journey. They are living now with their guilt and the waves of darkness which come up with it from the unconscious.

At first Jacob is totally unwilling to let Benjamin return to Egypt with his brothers: "You are robbing me of my children; Joseph is no more; Simeon is no more; and now you want to take Benjamin. All this I must bear." (Gen. 42:36). Not even Reuben's pledge that he will leave his own two sons with Jacob as hostages, to be put to death if he fails to return with Benjamin, reassures the heartbroken old man. But finally the hard reality of the famine forces Jacob to change his mind. There is no choice, and sadly and with foreboding the old father gives his consent for the brothers to return to Egypt with Benjamin.

Loaded with gifts, and with twice the amount of money they had found in their sacks, the brothers set off again for Egypt. When Joseph sees them coming, he instructs his servants to bring them to his house and prepare a feast for them. The brothers fear they are being taken to the palace to be punished for the money they discovered in their sacks, but, when they are assembled Joseph speaks to them kindly. He inquires after the welfare of their father, and when he sees Benjamin, his own mother's son, he is so overcome with emotion that he is again forced to leave the room to hide his tears: "He went into his room and there he wept." (Gen. 43:31). Then, having washed his face, he returns to the house and gives orders to serve the meal. After the meal is finished, Joseph gives the brothers the grain they need, but instructs his servants to place the money they paid for the grain, and his own personal silver cup in Benjamin's sack.

Again, the brothers set out on their way back to the land of Canaan, this time in high spirits. They feel their fears have not materialized, and they are returning safely with both the grain and Benjamin. Then suddenly they are stopped by Joseph's officer who, following Joseph's instructions, challenges them and accuses them of stealing the Prime Minister's cup. "Why did you reward good with evil? Is this not the one my lord uses for drinking and also for reading omens? What you have done is wrong." (Gen. 44:5).

The brothers protest their innocence, but when their sacks are searched, sure enough there is the missing cup in Benjamin's sack. At this the brothers rend their clothes in agony, and are led back to Joseph in the darkest despair. The night sea journey engulfs them again. Just as Joseph endured two dark sojourns—on the way to Egypt, and then, after thinking everything had worked out successfully, in Pharaoh's dungeon—so now the brothers pass through a second dark night of the soul.

With the brothers before him again, Joseph simulates great anger: "What is this deed you have done? Did you not know that a man such as I am is a reader of omens?" (Gen. 44:15). Judah now becomes the spokesman for the brothers. He cannot understand what has happened, but will do anything to ensure the safe return of Benjamin to Canaan: "Here we are then, my lord's slaves, we no less than the one in whose possession the cup was found." (Gen. 44:16). The brothers, who had sold Joseph as a slave, now themselves confront life as slaves. The night sea journey with all of its terrors is complete. They are forced to give up everything in life, even as Joseph was forced to give it up. They can hold on to nothing.

But Joseph pretends to refuse the offer of the brothers to remain as slaves. Only Benjamin shall remain, he says, for it was in his sack that the silver cup was found. Then Judah asks to speak to Joseph in private. He confides in him the whole story of the family. He tells him of his father, and of his father's bitter sorrow over the loss of Joseph. It is because of his old father's heart, Judah says, that Benjamin must return home. Judah concludes with a beautiful offer: "Let your servant stay, then, as my lord's slave in place of the boy, I implore you, and let the boy go back with his brothers. How indeed could I go back to my father and not have the boy with me? I could not bear to see the misery that would overwhelm my father." (Gen. 44:33-34).

Judah is the brother who was the original ringleader. He it was who suggested Joseph be sold as a slave and undermined Reuben's attempt to save him from the pit. Now all of Judah's arrogance and hatred are gone. He is willing to surrender his own life in order to spare his old father any further pain. His life has become for him as nothing, and he willingly offers to give it up for the sake of a higher value. Joseph can stand it no longer. He orders his attendants: "Let everyone leave me." (Gen. 45:1) Then, in what is one of the most moving and dramatic scenes of the Bible, he pours out his heart to his brothers: "I am Joseph. Is my father really still alive? ... I am your brother Joseph whom you sold into Egypt. But now, do not grieve, do not reproach yourselves for having sold me here, since God sent me before you to preserve your lives ... So it was not you who sent me here but God, and he has made me father to Pharaoh, lord of all his household and administrator of the whole land of Egypt." (Gen. 45:3-8) Then throwing his arms around Benjamin's neck he wept, and Benjamin also wept on his shoulder. He kissed each one of his brothers, and wept over them.

The American Revised Version of the Bible translates Gen. 45:7 in this way: "You meant it to me for evil, but God meant it for good." Joseph is free of vindictiveness toward his brothers because he sees his life in perspective; he perceives the pattern which has been at work in his life. We see the meaning of our lives when we see the pattern at work in them. When the pattern of our lives becomes clear to us, even the darkness and pain can be seen to have its proper place. In Joseph's case, the evil the brothers intended against him was intended by God for the purification of his soul, the destruction of his egocentricity, and for a way to bring him to Egypt where he would perform a great work. Yet this does not mean that everything always works out for the best. The evil the brothers intended could be used by God for good only because Joseph acquired the right attitude toward his life and became aware of his life pattern. Evil remains evil until man's consciousness grows because of it. Then God can use it for good.

Now there is a scene of great rejoicing as the brothers are reconciled to each other. Just as Jacob was reconciled with Esau, so now Joseph is reconciled with his brothers. The wholeness Joseph achieved within himself now extends to his relationships with them. The reconciliation is possible because of Joseph's highly developed consciousness, but also because of the change in the hearts of the brothers. Joseph tested his brothers to determine what was in their hearts, and when Judah was willing to be a slave so Benjamin could be spared, Joseph knew his brothers' hearts had found their way to God. His brothers were transformed, even as Joseph was transformed. To be sure, they are not as gifted as Joseph; they are not great administrators, nor do they interpret dreams or read omens. But in their own way they have grown greatly in psychological awareness and strength of character since that fateful day when they could not cope with their jealousy and fear and sold their brother as a slave. They too have undergone psychological development in the only way it is ever possible: a painful self-confrontation, a reckoning with the past, and a willingness to give up egocentricity in order to serve God.

PART THREE

The Reluctant Hero

CHAPTER EIGHT

Birth Of The Hero

Moses was a warrior, mystic, statesman, and prophet, rolled into one. Most men develop only one of these aspects of masculinity, but Moses developed all four. His relationship with God was profound and intimate, and his influence on the history of the people of Israel was second to none. Jacob knew God in his life from time to time. Like many of us, he was not a man to live with a constant sense of communion with God, but experienced Him in a series of separate crises. Joseph had a constant association with God through his dreams, but we do not hear of Joseph's having such direct encounters with the numinosum as came to Moses. Moses knew God "face to face."[1] He seemed to live his life with a constant communion and interaction with Him. But it was not always like this. Like Jacob and Joseph before him, Moses had to go through a time of great suffering and psychological development before he was ready to fulfill his divine calling.

The heroic nature of Moses' life is prefigured in the story of his birth. In the religious lore of mankind there are numerous stories of the births of heroes. In these tales certain typical motifs occur over and over again. To those who are familiar

---

[1](Ex. 33:11; Cf. Num. 14:14, Dt. 5:4, 34:10).

with stories of the births of heroes, these typical elements are easily recognized. As soon as they occur we can say, "Ah, this man may become a hero." The hero is the person whose consciousness becomes developed far beyond his fellows, whose psychological integration is being achieved, who fulfills in himself the divine plan and pattern for his life. By his greatly superior life and consciousness, the hero lifts the level of awareness, and influences the history of a whole people.

The story takes place in Egypt, many hundreds of years after Joseph, when a new Pharaoh came who did not know him. This new Pharaoh feared the power of the alien Hebrew people and decided to enslave them, lest they grow so strong they might become a threat to the kingdom. Perhaps he also wanted an excuse to increase the vast numbers of workers he needed for his many architectural projects, and so played on the idea of national security to justify what he did. But the Hebrews continued to multiply, even as slaves, and no doubt there was now great anger and discontent among them, so that Pharaoh continued to be afraid, and decreed that henceforth all male children among the Hebrews would be killed.

This cruel dictate was ruthlessly carried out, but one Hebrew mother, Jochebed (Ex. 6:20), was more resourceful and courageous than the rest. When her beautiful male child was born, she succeeded in hiding him for three months, and, when that was no longer possible, she made a tiny papyrus basket, placed the baby in it, and entrusted him to the River Nile. The child's older sister, Miriam, was sent to watch the basket from the banks of the river. Of course, had dangers arisen there is little she could have done, for the child might have been devoured by crocodiles, drowned in a whirlpool, swept out helplessly into the great Mediterranean, or floated endlessly until starvation came.

As fortune would have it, Pharaoh's daughter was bathing in the river when the tiny basket floated by. Curious, she sent her maids to fetch it, and when she beheld the tiny infant her heart was moved. "This is a child of one of the Hebrews," she remarked in astonishment. Miriam, who watched all this, ran out to her. "Shall I go and find you a nurse among the

Hebrew women to suckle the child for you?" she asked. (Ex. 2:6-7). At the bidding of Pharaoh's daughter, Miriam ran and brought the child's mother, who was paid by the Princess to suckle the young babe. When the child became a young lad he was taken into Pharaoh's own household, where the Princess treated him like her son. The child was named "Moses," because, she said, "I drew him out of the water." (Ex. 2:10)

It is typical that the future hero is born in the midst of great danger. In Moses' case other infants around him were being slaughtered by Pharaoh's soldiers, but he survived, thanks to the pluck of his mother and sister. In mythological lore, the hero is typically born in the midst of danger. The infant Hercules, for instance, is hated by Hera, who sends serpents into the child's crib to kill him; but the future hero strangles them with his sturdy infant hands. Asklepius, the Greek god of healing, is rescued from death at the last moment when Apollo snatches the unborn infant from his dead mother's body just before flames engulf it on a great funeral pyre. The most striking Biblical comparison is Jesus, who survives when Herod's soldiers, like Pharaoh's, come through the town of Bethlehem slaughtering the children. Thanks to the intervention of angels, who warn his earthly father, Joseph, the life of the infant Jesus is saved.

It is also typical of the hero that the newborn infant is an abandoned child. In Moses' story his desperate mother decides to trust him to the elements rather than see him face certain death by continuing to care for him herself. So the infant drifts perilously down the River Nile in his tiny basket, exposed to the hazards and uncertainties of nature. But the river is kind to him. He is not swept away, or drowned, or pulled out to sea; instead the currents of the stream carry the babe safely to the area where Pharaoh's daughter is bathing. A parallel story in mythology is the tale of Romulus and Remus, the heroes of ancient Rome who were left to drift on the river Tiber, but were rescued by the great she-wolf who suckled and raised them. Jesus also was abandoned, in a sense, since there was no room for him in the inn. As a consequence, his birth took place amidst nature in the stable surrounded by the animals. It seems as though the future hero's hold on life is greater than most people's. He survives where others would have perished.

This survival is due to the special care given the child by nature, or by divine forces, or both. In Moses' case, it was as though the River Nile itself was kind to him and guided him to the right spot. Romulus and Remus, as we noted, were raised by a she-wolf, and Jesus found friendly support from the animals in the stable, and direct divine assistance from the angelic host who, in a series of dreams to the Magi and to Joseph, averted the dangers threatening the newborn infant.

Finally we have the motif of the hero's dual parents.[2] Moses, for instance, had his ordinary Hebrew parents, and his royal Egyptian family. Countless heroes of myth and legend have a similar motif. Oedipus, for instance, is raised by the simple peasant couple in the mountains, but also has his royal lineage, and Asclepius is raised by the centaur Chiron, but has Apollo for a heavenly father. But Jesus is the greatest example. He has Mary and Joseph, his earthly parents, but he is also the child of the Holy Spirit, and lives with the awareness of his heavenly origins. In the story of the boy Jesus in the Temple, when Mary and Joseph had to hunt to find him, Jesus answers them, astonished that they did not understand, "Wist ye not that I must be about my Father's business?" (Luke 2:49 KJV)

The motif of the dual parentage helps us see the meaning of the hero. It is as though the hero derives his extraordinary consciousness from a royal or divine source, as well as an ordinary, human one. He is a twice-born person, whose personality has its source in the archetypal spiritual world, and is not moulded simply by human conventions and his ordinary surroundings. Psychologically speaking, the hero is a person who lives in close contact with the inner world of the unconscious and its spiritual powers. This brings the hero stories closer to us. For, while history records the lives and deeds of its great heroes, all of us have the potentiality to become the hero, each in his or her own way. As soon as a creative contact

---

[2]Cf. the article by Esther Harding, in Chapter One of "The Well-Tended Tree" published by the C. G. Jung Foundation, Hilde Kirsch, Ed.

with the inner world is established, the potentiality for the heroic life has been created.

A study of comparative mythology highlights the archetypal features of the story of the birth of Moses. As we have seen, it is typical of a certain type of story. But this does not necessarily deny the historicity of Moses or the essentials of the Biblical account. In certain people, the archetypal or mythological background of life emerges and is lived out in their lives. This is what gives them an extraordinary quality. So the fact that there are archetypal elements in the stories of Jacob, Joseph, and Moses does not deny the historicity of these Biblical characters, but speaks to their reality as people in whom the divine lived.

The infant Moses had the birth of a hero, but this did not guarantee he would become a hero. Before the seed of a potential hero in him could develop, the young Moses had to undergo a process of psychological development and transformation. As with Jacob and Joseph before him, his egocentricity had to be destroyed, so that his life could be moulded by the Greater Will within him. How this happened will take up the rest of our narrative.

CHAPTER NINE

The Making Of A Hero

When we next see Moses he is a young man. Although he was raised in Pharaoh's household, he also was aware of his Hebrew origins, for one day we are told that he set out to visit his countrymen. We can only guess why he did this. Perhaps he was searching for his own identity, for part of our personal sense of identity comes from knowing our ancestral roots and our place in history. Or perhaps he was just curious, and wanted to see how things were in the world beyond the palace. Curiosity, as we shall see, was strong in Moses' character; it is also one of the greatest impulses pulling us into life and our psychological development. When he does find his countrymen, Moses is shocked at the hard life they are leading, and filled with anger and indignation at their lot. Suddenly he sees an Egyptian task-master beating one of the Hebrew slaves. After glancing around him to be sure no one is looking, he sets upon the Egyptian and beats him furiously until he lies dead on the ground.

Our reactions toward Moses' deed are mixed. In a way we are pleased by his capacity for righteous indignation, but we also wonder if a lot of guilt was not mixed into it. After all, Moses was not suffering any of the hardships of his people. He was living in a fine palace, while his countrymen were living as slaves. It is certain that his act was a rash one, dictated by an eruption of emotion. When a man goes into a rage so great that he kills someone, as Moses did, he is possessed by something. He does not have the emotion, the emotion has him. In terms of masculine psychology this often has to do with his inner feminine side. It is as though a woman inside of him throws a match into the gasoline and he erupts in fire. This kind of aggression is not the controlled aggression which is one hallmark of a truly masculine person. So Moses' rash act suggests that, as a man, he was still unformed and this is why his action accomplishes nothing. Just the same, there is a kind of nobility in the young man which is beginning to show itself. There is also an impressive demonstration of physical prowess, and of budding social compassion, qualities which emerge later in Moses and distinguish his life.

Moses' murder of the Egyptian is not appreciated by his fellow countrymen. Returning the next day to the area in which the murder was committed, Moses sees two Hebrews quarreling and tries to settle the dispute between them, but his overtures as judge and peacemaker are rejected. One of them challenges him with, "And who appointed you to be prince over us, and judge? Do you intend to kill me as you killed the Egyptian?" Moses is frightened, for he realizes that the murder has been seen. He thinks to himself, "Clearly that business has come to light." (Ex. 2:14).

It is worth noting that Moses speaks of "that business." "That business" is murder, but Moses cannot bring himself to use the word. This suggests that he is not yet as psychologically honest as Jacob was when he acknowledged that he was cheating his father, and did not use any euphemisms.

When Moses realizes his crime has been discovered, he decides to flee for fear of punishment from Pharaoh. Notice that there is no thought or plan in his mind to remain in Egypt to try to do something for his countrymen, nor even to return later to try to help them. Moses' murder of the Egyptian may have been partly motivated by righteous indignation, but it takes more than this to make someone a helper of men and a reformer of society. He does not yet have the maturity of personality to do anything truly helpful for his people, and, when the chips are down, Moses winds up thinking only of saving his own skin.

So off Moses runs into the wilderness. Like Jacob before him, he is an exile. Like Joseph, Moses also gives up everything: his favored position in the palace, his friends and protectors, his guarantee of a future in a privileged position in society. We have no details of what Moses was experiencing inwardly on his flight through the wilderness, but we can imagine that he felt the same kind of desolation, loneliness, and anxiety which had swept over Jacob and Joseph. And he was no doubt hounded and tortured, not only by the outer dangers he was facing, but also from within, from those voices inside him which must have reproached him for his rash act, and accused him of a cowardly flight. He was pursued by the furies, and those who have endured psychological agony know that such psychic terrors and pain are greater than physical pain.

Moses' journey through the wilderness is another version of the night sea journey experience which Jacob and Joseph endured. He went through an inner personal hell as well as an outer wilderness. The experience occurs to all three of our heroes, because it is typical of those who are called upon to undergo marked psychological development that such a painful, dark journey must be made.

When at long last Moses arrives in the land of Midian, east of the land of Egypt, he finds his way to a well. The priest of the region lives nearby, and his seven daughters come to the well to draw water, but are set upon by rough shepherds who drive them away. Moses leaps to the defense of the girls, scatters the ruffians, and draws the water for them. Again we see Moses' capacity for righteous anger and his sense of social injustice, but this time he acts in a more mature way. He does not injure or kill any of the shepherds, and stays on to help the girls with the task of drawing the water. We also see evidence again that Moses is a man of prodigious physical strength, for though the shepherds outnumber him they flee in terror.

In the life of Jacob we saw how important it was that he loved Rachel so personally and intensely; this gave evidence that Jacob was a man in whom the feminine, eros side of life was richly developed. In Joseph's life we also saw the highly developed eros function in his faithfulness to Potiphar, and his tenderness toward his brothers. In Moses we see the same eros development. His act on behalf of the girls is typical for a man who, in addition to his masculine side, has a deep appreciation for the feminine.

The complete personality achieves a balance and integration of the masculine and the feminine. We all carry within us both of these opposites, but men and women relate to them differently. Generally a man will identify with his masculinity, and wear his femininity on the inside; a woman conversely. But if wholeness is to be established, a man must relate to the feminine side of himself as well as the masculine side. In masculine psychology, the masculine ego cannot live successfully without support from the feminine unconscious. A man develops the hero within himself not only by performing feats of masculinity, but also by his creative relatedness to the feminine, for without this his masculinity becomes boorish or brutal.

The masculine and the feminine are like two great poles around which all psychic life flows. In Chinese thought they are represented as the eternal Yang and Yin, the bright, hot masculine element, and the dark, cool feminine element. As these two forces interact, so all life is shaped, and the Way of Heaven itself (Tao) is determined by the inner-relationship of Yang and Yin.

Dr. Esther Harding[1] suggests that the masculine is like the light of the sun, and the feminine like the light of the moon. In the bright light of sunlight, everything is seen clearly and things are easily differentiated from one another. In the light of the moon, things are blended together and seen as a whole. Masculine consciousness tends to perceive things brightly, to focus upon them intently, to differentiate one thing from another. Feminine consciousness is more diffused, and is likely to become aware of many things which are obscured in the intense light of the masculine. But both elements are necessary if wholeness is to be established, and one great task of in-

---

[1] *Woman's Mysteries,* published by G. P. Putnam's Sons, 1971, p. 28.

dividuation is to develop in such a way that the masculine
and feminine within us work creatively and in harmony.

Jacob, Joseph, and Moses are all examples of masculine
men in whom the feminine has also been appreciated and integrated. Perhaps the greatest example of all, however, is Jesus,
a man who was remarkable for his relationships with the feminine. In his day it was unheard of for a man to have women
for friends, yet Jesus numbered many women among his closest
associates, and did not hesitate to speak with them person to
person. [In his own personality, the feminine qualities of eros,
relatedness, compassion, and healing share an equal place with
the masculine qualities of aggression and forcefulness.]

The young girls are pleased with Moses, naturally enough,
and promptly take him home with them to their father, Reuel,
or Jethro as he is called in another tradition, who welcomes
the young man to his household, and offers him one of his
daughters in marriage. Moses accepts (which must have made
the others frightfully jealous) and settles down to the comfortable
life of a shepherd. Apparently Reuel had seven daughters but
no sons, a sad plight for a shepherd who needed help with
his flocks, and he evidently was overjoyed to have his vigorous
young son-in-law remain with him. The wilderness experience
is soon left far behind Moses, and so are the memories of
Egypt and the suffering of his people. Moses settles down to
a pleasant existence, surrounded by his new-found and loving
family. He begins to act like many a man has acted before
and after him. If he had lived today we would no doubt find
him somewhere in suburbia, going to the office during the week,
mowing the lawn on Saturdays, and taking the family on outings
in the family camper on Sundays. He has found the "good
life," and desires nothing more than his family, his work, and
the ordinary pleasures of life.

This is all very nice, but if something had not happened
he would not have become the Moses whom we remember
today. Most of us try to live life on exactly the level on which
Moses is living. We want the good life and our comforts, and
people around who love us, but when we get what we want,
the danger is that all growth will stop. Maybe this is when
God needs the devil to stir things up. Something must happen

to upset the normal, pleasant course of life, and get us once more on our way: an illness, a catastrophe, difficulty with our marriage, a troubling psychological symptom, or sometimes just an unwanted, insatiable "divine restlessness." It may be that God permits evil precisely so that life will not get so comfortable for us that we fall psychologically and spiritually asleep. In Goethe's play *Faust,* Mephistopheles, who describes himself as "part of that force which would do evil, yet forever works the good,"[2] complains that no one appreciates him. "Why," he declares, "if it were not for me nothing would ever happen!" Moses needed something to happen if his growth was to continue, but in this case God did not need the help of the devil, but confronted Moses directly. God had other plans for him, as Moses, to his dismay, is soon to discover.

---

[2] *Faust*, Part One, p. 49, The Library of Liberal Arts.

CHAPTER TEN

The Reluctant Hero

One day when Moses is with his flocks, he comes to the other side of a nearby mountain, Horeb, also called Sinai, the famous mountain of Old Testament history. Here he is astonished at a strange sight: a bush which is burning, but is not consumed in the fire. Overwhelmed by curiosity, Moses approaches the fiery bush to see what this strange matter is all about.

Giving in to his curiosity was the decisive step in Moses' life. We have already seen the change curiosity made in his life when he set out to find his countrymen and ended by murdering the Egyptian taskmaster. Curiosity, the desire to know, is a powerful instinct, often used by God to draw us into life and our individuation. But it is also a troublesome instinct. If Moses had not been so curious, had he, perhaps, let caution have the upper hand, he might have been able to stay in his comfortable way of life as a simple shepherd in the land of Midian. But, like Adam and Eve, his curiosity got the upper hand and as a result he became involved in something of which he had never dreamed, even in his wildest imagination.

It is often this way with those who become involved in their own inner journeys, since it begins either with necessity (because there is no other way out of some life impasse) or with curiosity (I wonder what is down there for me in that strange inner world?). In either case one gets "caught"; that is, involved in a process of growing and searching from which there is no escape.

When Moses is near the strange burning bush he suddenly hears a Voice call out from it: "Moses, Moses!" Startled, Moses answers, "Here I am." The Voice continues, "Come no nearer. Take off your shoes, for the place on which you stand is holy ground. I am the God of your father, the God of Abraham, the God of Isaac and the God of Jacob." (Ex. 3:4-6).

No one today has ever known of a bush which burned but was not consumed in the fire, nor of a voice speaking out of the flames. We do know, however, that there is a type of inner experience which has this kind of numinosity and compelling power, and that there is such an experience as being called from within to a special mission in life. It is not unusual, for instance, to have dreams with images such as Moses' burning bush, and such dreams always speak of a call from a deeper level within the personality to a new life mission or journey. Moses' inner experience is personified in the story in this dramatic way. As with many Biblical stories, it is not necessary to take the story literally to get at its truth, since it is the psychological or spiritual truth which matters.

The Voice from the fire identifies itself as the God of Moses' long forgotten ancestors. Abraham and Jacob could have warned Moses that this God was not to be taken lightly, and that He had a way of completely changing a person's life. Abraham heard this Voice and went on the long journey from Ur to Canaan as a result. Jacob heard the Voice in his dream of the ladder reaching up to heaven and it shook his egocentricity to the core. Now Moses is being given this birthright of his ancestors: direct relationship with the Numinosum.

Up until now God had perhaps been known to Moses only by hearsay, or as an almost lost tradition among his enslaved countrymen. Now he will know God directly; God will no longer be a Power in whom he believes in a vague kind of way, or through tradition, but a reality which he experiences and with Whom he interacts. When we believe in something, it is as though we have made up our minds to think in a certain way. When we have experienced a reality, however, then we *know* it. As C. G. Jung once remarked when asked if he believed in God: "I *know*. I don't need to believe, I know."[1] From this time on Moses will know God; the knowledge will not make his life comfortable, but it will make it supremely meaningful.

The ground on which Moses is standing is holy ground. This means that it was charged with numinosity. In the Bible, if something is holy it is numinous. As we have seen, God's holiness, or numinosity, is His chief characteristic. There are powerful psychological experiences which have this kind of numinosity. The ego confronts some Center of unity from the inner world and it is a numinous experience. When such an experience comes to us, we are never quite the same again.

Moses' reaction is natural enough: he hides his face, unable to look at this awesome sight. What the Voice says next must have increased Moses' fear even more. God proclaims in the Voice from the burning bush that He is confronting him this way because He wants him to go to the land of Egypt. There he is to tell Pharaoh to let the people of Israel go.

What a preposterous idea! Not only is Pharaoh certain to ridicule the idea that he should let his slaves go free, but Moses is wanted there for murder. Moses replies incredulously: "Who am I to go to Pharaoh and bring the sons of Israel out of Egypt?" (Ex. 3:11).

But Moses is being called upon by God to be the hero, and this always means to accomplish the difficult, even seemingly impossible task, whether it is an inward task or an outer one. We are all called upon to become heroes, each in our own way. The call to psychological growth is universal, and while not all of us will become a Moses, we are all called upon to accomplish our own particular life task. It always involves freeing our slaves from Pharaoh, for Pharaoh, psychologically, is the tyrant of the ego, the demonic hold our egocentricity has on us which enslaves our true personality. The call from God is to confront this terrible tyrant and do battle with him. This is always a heroic undertaking, but one from which we

---

[1]BBC filmed interview with C. G. Jung, 1958.

cannot escape once God has laid His hand upon us. Like Moses, we may be incredulous. "Why should I give up my comfortable and secure way of life and go on a journey fraught with psychological dangers and uncertainties?" we may ask.

Moses does not want the hero task and comes up with a series of excuses why he should not go to Egypt as God wants him to. First he says he does not know what to say if people ask him who has sent him. God answers this by revealing to Moses His name: "I Am who I Am. This is what you must say to the sons of Israel: I Am has sent me to you." (Ex. 3:14).

Moses has revealed to him what Jacob was not allowed to know: the name of God. One's name reveals the inner essence of personality, and God's name in the Old Testament reveals that God is beyond time. He is the eternally present, and is not conditioned or bound by past and future as is the ego. His mode of existence is not like ours, bound and limited as we are by a sense of space and time. He is the great "I Am," the numinous reality which a human being can confront, but can never rationally comprehend.

A second excuse Moses uses is that he is poor as a man of speech: "But, my Lord, never in my life have I been a man of eloquence, either before or since you have spoken to your servant. I am a slow speaker and not able to speak well." God retorts testily: "Who gave man his mouth? Who makes him dumb or deaf, gives him sight or leaves him blind? Is it not I, Yahweh? Now go, I shall help you to speak and tell you what to say." (Ex. 4:10–12).

Later, in another section, God declares that He will send Moses' brother, Aaron, to accompany him, for Aaron is fluent in speech. But it is interesting to note that, as the story progresses, we find Moses makes his own speeches, and does not need Aaron to do the talking for him. Once he has accepted his inner calling, his speech problem vanishes, which suggests that his speech defect was a neurotic symptom brought about by the repression of his psychological development. When the

---

²The priestly source often has Aaron, who was a priest, doing the talking for Moses, but in the most ancient sources Moses speaks for himself.

necessity for his inner journey was accepted and his larger personality potential was unleashed, his symptom vanished. Quite often our blocks are not the result of past trauma, but result from the damming up of the personality, that is, from our inability to move into the future. The cure then comes about when we accept the necessity for psychological growth and move ahead. It is another example of the importance of the teleological factor in our psychology.

Eventually Moses exhausts all of the excuses he can think of and declares in frustration: "If it please you, my Lord, send anyone you will!" At this the Bible tells us: "The anger of Yahweh blazed out against Moses." (Ex. 4:13–14). Then and only then, does Moses reluctantly take up his task.

This is an example of what we can call the wrath, or the dark side, of God. There is a dark side to this matter of spiritual growth, for it will not be denied. If we insist on turning it aside, once we have been called upon to make the inner journey, it may turn negative and destructive. The same process which can lead to wholeness and consciousness can also poison and destroy us if we try to avoid it. Many people find themselves in Moses' predicament: only when they are forced to their journey out of fear of the consequences if they do not go, do they begin their psychological development. For good reason the Bible declares, "The fear of the Lord is the beginning of wisdom." (Psalm 111:10 and Proverbs 9:10, KJV.) Moses wisely decides that the only thing to do is to obey this frightening, demanding Voice which will not be turned aside.

Moses was indeed a reluctant hero, but once he undertook his journey he did not look back. Jesus once said, "Once the hand is laid on the plough, no one who looks back is fit for the kingdom of God." (Luke 9:62). Moses, having put his hand to the plough, did not turn away from it. If Jacob's great psychological virtue was his self-honesty, and Joseph's his power to interpret dreams, Moses' was his unswerving perseverance and constancy of purpose once his life task had been accepted.

The remainder of Moses' story has both an outer and an inner meaning. Outwardly we may take the story of the freeing of the people of Israel from slavery as history. But it also has psychological significance, for the people of Israel in slavery are symbolic of our own nature, enslaved to the Pharaoh-like tyrant of our egocentricity. The hero is the one who brings about freedom. To work toward wholeness is to become increasingly a free person. To live life out of our Center, rather than enslaved by our egocentricity, is to begin to be free.

But it can be frightening to live as a free person. There is always a part of us which prefers the life of a slave to the life of freedom, as Dostoevsky showed in his famous Grand Inquisitor scene.[3] If we are free we must act in a mature way, accepting reponsibility for our happiness or unhappiness, success or failure. A free person must pull his own oar in life, and give up childishness and dependency. He must make conscious choices, and not simply follow what everyone else is doing. It often seems easier to remain a slave. Then we can complain about our condition, blame our failures and unhappiness on others, and avoid the burdensome responsibility of freedom.

This is the way the people of Israel often felt. Moses finally succeeded in leading them out of Egypt, but whenever the going became difficult, the people became angry and wanted to return to their former slavery. These people had a slave mentality and were not able to undergo the rigors of psychological development. Unlike Esau and Joseph's brothers, they rejected the way of individuation. To be sure, they did not return to Egypt, because God and Moses would not let them, but they remained slaves in their minds nonetheless. They finally perished in the desert; because of their lack of resolution God would not allow them to enter the promised land, but waited for their descendants, who were born free in the wilderness and valued the joy of freedom more than the security of slavery.

We find this same flight from freedom in many areas of life today. In the cure of souls, for instance, it is not unusual for a person to reach a point where a new and free life may become possible, only to have that person suddenly abandon the whole process, as though the resulting freedom would be too much to bear. The same thing often occurs in marriages, in which one, or perhaps both of the partners live within a box. Many marriages are characterized by torturous roles the

---

[3] Dostoevsky, *The Brothers Karamazov*, Book V, Chapt. 5.

man or woman is compelled to play in order to maintain a stultifying relationship. It is possible to break out of such fixed roles and stereotypes, but some people prefer to slip back into the old structure rather than to face freedom; it is less frightening than facing life in a mature way.

Moses became a free man. The whole range of his personality was being expressed in his life. His egocentricity had been replaced by a tremendous ego strength which enabled him to talk with God "face to face." But his freedom is not to be confused with license. Moses was free as long as he served God. His ego was the servant of the Larger Life and Will within him. He left the personal pleasure principle and hedonistic way of life behind him in the land of Midian when he set out to free his people from Pharaoh. If we want license to live out all our whims and desires, we need to understand that this is not freedom, but merely another version of egocentricity and slavery. The Book of Common Prayer expresses it well when, speaking of God, it says ... "whose service is perfect freedom."

True freedom makes tremendous demands upon us. Most of us, like Moses, resist the call to the free life. He was a reluctant hero who became free only when he feared God more than he feared Pharaoh. For most of us this is also the way it will be. We will not give up our comfort, security, and the pleasures of an egocentric life until we are forced by God to do so. Then, unwillingly, we may set out on our journey to liberate ourselves from our personal Pharaoh's Egypt. But in the end we are glad that we did. We look back on our old life in the pleasant suburbia of Midian and rejoice that we left it for the hardships of the journey. For a journey with God is the only real source of satisfaction there is, and a life of freedom, no matter how demanding, the only life worth living.

PART FOUR

In Defense
Of Adam And Eve

CHAPTER ELEVEN

What's In A Myth?

Our studies of Jacob, Joseph, and Moses showed similar patterns in their lives. It is as though there was a destiny which awaited each one of them, and this destiny was fulfilled when their egocentricity was eliminated, and their lives reorganized around a divine center. This involved them in a continual growth in consciousness, and an expansion of personality. The Bible as a whole, as well as these selected stories, can be understood as the unfolding of man's psychological development and spiritual awareness. How this process began is our point of interest in the next story we are to consider: the story of Adam and Eve.

The Bible contains two different creation stories. The first is in the first chapter of the Book of Genesis, and the second, the Adam and Eve story, begins with Genesis 2:4. The first story is much more sophisticated and philosophical. Obviously some keen minds originated this poetic and powerful declaration of how God went about creating the earth. It is also a much later version, thought to have been written by the priestly class around the year 600 B.C. In comparison, the Adam and Eve story is primitive and childlike, and certainly much older. In fact, no one knows how old this ancient creation story is. It must have been circulated by word of mouth long before anyone thought of writing it down.

But in spite of the childlike nature of the Adam and Eve creation story, it is the one which has had the greater influence upon the thinking of Western man. We all admire the beauty of the Genesis One account, but the story of the Garden of Eden is the one which has gripped our imagination and shaped our psychology.

The power of the story of the Garden of Eden comes from its mythlike quality. Genesis One reads like a kind of scientific statement, but the Adam and Eve story is obviously a myth. In our culture to call something a myth is, in the minds of most people, to disparage the story. A myth, for most of us, means something that is illusory, foolish, or false. This view of myth comes from our ignorance about the meaning of mythology, and is most unfortunate, for a myth is a particular form of story which conveys powerful psychological and spiritual truths. Let's take a look for a moment at what is involved in a myth, beginning with a glance at two commonly held ideas about mythology, and then looking at the contribution of psychology to our understanding.

The prevailing view of mythology is that it is a kind of pre-science. It is commonly supposed that primitive people tried to explain things by means of myths before they had science, that it is therefore a kind of childlike, pre-scientific way of thinking and is useless for modern people with their superior intellectual development.

A second view of mythology is that myths are elaborations of historical facts. Hercules, for instance, may have been a person who actually lived at one time, who did certain heroic things in his lifetime, and around whom imagination eventually spun a fanciful web of tales.

Psychology, however, sees in mythology statements from the unconscious about man's deepest psychological processes. The psychological viewpoint understands myths as spontaneously formulated representations in story form of universal patterns of psychological development which have not reached consciousness. Myths are the language of the archetypes. They are stories in which the universal, or archetypal, developments taking place in man are portrayed. They are not consciously contrived; that is, no one sat down to think them up, but they have found their way into consciousness from the unconscious, perhaps evolving over many years, but always being essentially shaped by the imagery of the inner world. Myths are to the human race as a whole as dreams are to the individual: pictorial representations of what is taking place in the soul.

The archetypal aspect of myths accounts for their universality. Students of mythology discover that mythological motifs are the same the world over. The cast of characters has different names, the cultural settings are different, but the mythological motifs are strikingly similar. One student of mythology, for instance, Joseph Campbell, has collected stories of the hero from all over the world. He has found them so strikingly similar that he called his book *The Hero With A Thousand Faces*, and terms the story of the hero the great "Mono-Myth." Psychologically understood, the hero myth has to do with the emergence of the ego out of the matrix of original unconsciousness, and the development of the ego in accordance with the power of the total personality.

Once we understand this, our attitude toward a myth can change. Myths can then be appreciated as exceedingly valuable stories, expressing, as nothing else does, truths about man's psychological and spiritual situation. Myths are especially important since it has been shown that each individual today repeats, in his or her own psychological development, all the evolutionary progressions of mankind before him. A modern man must go through an ego development analogous to the development primitive man underwent during many centuries. So myths have a way of recurring in the lives of people today. Sometimes we find individuals who are living out a particular myth. We often find elements of mythologies in our dreams; in fact, an understanding of dreams is impossible without a thorough grounding in mythology. Far from being unimportant, a proper understanding of myth is essential for an understanding of the human soul, both past and present.

To call the story of Adam and Eve a myth, therefore, is not to disparage it in any way, but rather to look at it as a uniquely important kind of story. The historicity of the story need not concern us; the important thing is the psychological and spiritual truths which we can expect to emerge from it. It is an especially important myth for us because it deals with the most fundamental question of human life: of man's relationship to God, of the role of evil in life, and of the reason behind man's painful existence.

To approach this story in the right way, however, we must let the story speak to us. This is a little hard to do since most of us have already been exposed to a vast amount of theologizing about it. Precisely because of its powerful mythological character, this story has fascinated man's mind for thousands of years and innumerable interpretations of the story have been made. We are no doubt familiar with the prevailing view of the story: that it tells of man's original sin of disobedience to God, and of the way man brought evil into his own life. This view, which we can call the traditional view, is widely held, but is not the only way to understand the story. Later I will comment on some other interpretations of the story, and, of course, I have my own view to suggest.

We need to remember that the story itself contains no interpretation; in the Bible the story is simply told. It has much the same status as a dream. A dream unfolds before our eyes; it is up to us to listen carefully to the dream, and be faithful to its every detail, so that the correct interpretation of the dream may evolve in our minds. The story of Adam and Eve is much the same. Dreamlike, it unfolds before our eyes. Every detail is important. It gives us no fixed interpretation, but it does invite us to ponder its meaning. With this perspective to guide us, let us look again at this ancient tale, and see if it will speak to us anew about our psychological and spiritual situation, and that ancient and crucial question of our relationship to God.

CHAPTER TWELVE

The Original Man

According to our ancient story tellers, the first thing the Lord God created was a man. He made him out of the dust of the earth and then breathed into the man's nostrils the breath of life, and in this way the man became a living being.

This original man is a composite being. His nature is of the dust of the earth, but he is enlivened by the presence within him of the breath of God Himself. Matter and spirit, earth and heaven, the mortal and the Divine, are thus intermingled to make this first man. The image the story uses is anthropomorphic: God, like a great giant, molding a figurine with His hands, then breathing life into the doll-like figure with His breath. But the spiritual truth is profound: man is made up of pairs of opposites.

Next God planted a garden in which the man He had made could live. The garden lay in a remarkable place called Eden. Every kind of beautiful tree and fruit was in the garden, and from the garden flowed a river, which branched out in four directions to make four rivers which watered all the land roundabout. The garden had a center point, and here were two special trees: the tree of life, and the tree of the knowledge of good and evil.

The Garden of Eden suggests a mandala, because of its

central point with the remarkable trees, and the river flowing from it. A mandala is a concentric design which represents or symbolizes wholeness. In a mandala everything is grouped around a center. The shape of the mandala is circular, or sometimes, square. In a circle, every point on the circumference is equidistant from the center, so the shape of the circle suggests balance and completeness.

Mandalas are represented in religious art all over the world. Many Christian churches, for instance, have mandalas in the form of the so-called Rose Windows of circular design. Because of the mandala shape of the garden, we are met immediately with the suggestion that the story is about wholeness; how man was originally contained within it, but then fell away from it.

The trees are of special interest to us. The tree of life is something with which we are familiar from our study of mythological lore. In shamanism, for instance, as we observed earlier, there is a tree at the center of the earth. This is known as the Cosmic Tree and it reaches from earth to heaven. The shaman, who knows how to find it, uses it to make his ascent to commune with the spiritual world above. The tree of the knowledge of good and evil, however, claims the forefront of the story of the Garden of Eden. It becomes the focal point because it is the only thing in the garden which is prohibited. The man may eat of the fruit of any of the trees in the garden except this one, for God has said that on the day he eats of it he shall die.

The man has a beautiful place in which to dwell, but he finds it is lonely there in the garden by himself, so God creates the wild beasts and the birds of heaven. Each of these is brought to the man to name, which must have been rather fun for him, but when all this is done, none of these wild creatures is found to be a suitable mate for him. So God causes the man to fall into a deep sleep, and, taking from him one of his ribs, makes of it a woman.

The tale, of course, is told from a masculine perspective. A woman has told me another version: in the beginning God made man. Then He said to Himself, "I can do better than that." So he made Eve! The important thing to note, however, is that this first man, whom we may call Adam (which means "man") was androgynous,[1] that is, masculine and feminine at the same time.

We have already observed in our studies of Jacob, Joseph, and Moses, that each man contains a feminine element, and each woman a masculine element, so that the total personality is masculine and feminine. Mythology hints at this psychological fact in its many descriptions of an original man who was both male and female. In Adam's case, Eve was contained within him and was made into a separate being so he would not be alone. The Bible adds, "For this reason, a man must leave his father and mother and be joined to his wife, and the two will become one body." (Eph. 5:31–32). The image is that of the two halves who seek for each other in order to restore a lost totality. Man seeks woman and woman seeks man, as though they are looking for their lost completeness. For this reason, St. Paul refers to the union of male and female in sexuality as a "mystery." It is a way of saying that the psychic image behind sexual desire is the yearning for wholeness.

This motif of the androgynous man is found in myths all over the world. Plato gives us a good example in the *Symposium*. According to the ancient Greek myth about which Plato tells us, the original man "was round, his back and sides forming a circle; and he had four hands and four feet, one head with two faces, looking opposite ways ... also four ears, two privy members, and the remainder to correspond." These original spherical beings proved to be so strong that they challenged the gods for supremacy, and Zeus, to humble them and ensure the continued supremacy of the gods, cut them in two. Out of the severed halves came man and woman, as we know them, but these two beings were immediately beset with the most terrible longing to re-establish their lost totality. "Each of us when separated", Plato says, "having one side only ... is but indenture of a man, and he is always looking for his other half."[2]

We find the same thought in the ancient Chinese oracle

---

[1] From the Greek: Andros—man, gynos—woman.
[2] From the Modern Library *Plato*, p. 354.

book *The I Ching*, which refers to the "two souls active in the body of man, one masculine, and the other feminine."[3] Of these two natures, the masculine is the active, light principle, and the feminine the downward moving, dark principle. If at the death of the body the ego has not succeeded in reuniting these two halves of one totality, the masculine part flies upward for a brief sojourn in heaven, and the feminine part is dissolved back into the earth.

Poets and philosophers have also grasped this mystery of the original, androgynous nature of man. Consider this quotation from the Russian religious philosopher, Nicholas Berdyaev:[4] "Man is not only a sexual but a bisexual being, combining the masculine and the feminine principles in himself in different proportions and often in fierce conflict. A man in whom the feminine principle was completely absent would be an abstract being ... a woman in whom the masculine principle was completely absent would not be a personality ... It is only the union of these two principles that constitutes a complete human being. Their union is realized in every man and every woman within their bisexual androgynous nature, and it also takes place through the intercommunion between the two natures, the masculine and the feminine."

Now that Adam is happy with his mate, Eve, and the problem of his loneliness is solved, God leaves them alone in the Garden to enjoy themselves. They can, as we observed, do anything they like, except eat of the fruit of the tree of the knowledge of good and evil. All might have gone well except that there is in the Garden with Adam and Eve an extremely subtle creature, the serpent. No sooner has God left the scene than the serpent approaches Eve and says to her, "Did God really say you were not to eat from any of the trees in the garden?" Eve dutifully repeats God's instructions, "You must not eat it, nor touch it, under pain of death." The serpent exclaims, "No! You will not die! God knows in

---

[3] The Nature of the *I Ching*, Poncé, p. 42–43.
[4] *The Destiny of Man*, Nicholas Berdyaev, Harper Torchbook, pp. 62–63.

fact that on the day you eat it your eyes will be opened and you will be like gods, knowing good and evil." (Gen. 3:1–5).

Here, of course, is the famous temptation from the serpent which caused the fall of man. The problem, many have suggested, is that Adam and Eve did not obey God. Had they only obeyed Him all would have been well, and God's perfect creation would not have been spoiled, neither would sin, guilt, and death have been brought into man's life. But a close examination of the story suggests that the motive of Eve for eating forbidden fruit was not disobedience as such but curiosity, the desire to know, and the dsire for power, to "be like gods."

For of course Eve did eat of the forbidden fruit, and having eaten, she soon persuaded Adam to eat of it too. And even as the serpent had said, "Then the eyes of both of them were opened and they realized that they were naked." (Gen. 3:7). To say "the eyes of both of them were opened" suggests that a light has dawned in them; they have become conscious. But the consciousness which has come to them is painful. For the first time they realize their sexuality; they are shy about their bodies, and sew fig leaves together to make clothes for themselves.

The presence of the serpent in the Garden is an important matter. It is not hard to imagine that the serpent is a personification of a voice within Adam and Eve, that he symbolizes an urge from within toward knowledge and personal power. He can be taken, psychologically, as we shall see, as a personification of the urge toward psychological development.

It is also important to notice that Adam and Eve are not responsible for the presence of the serpent in the Garden. No one has ever suggested that this serpent, who, after all, instigated the eating of the forbidden fruit, was created by the man and woman. He must, then, have been created by God, a point we shall return to shortly.

It is not very long before Adam and Eve hear God walking through the garden. Guiltily, they run and hide. As soon as God realizes the man and woman are hiding from Him, His suspicions are aroused. "Where are you?" he demands of Adam. Adam replies, "I was afraid because I was naked, so I hid."

"Who told you that you were naked?" God asks suspiciously. This question is presumably met with silence. God continues, "Have you been eating of the tree I forbade you to eat?" (Gen. 3:9–11).

The jig is up now, and Adam replies with an all too human response, "It was the woman you put with me; she gave me the fruit, and I ate it." God says to the woman, "What is this you have done?" Eve replies weakly, "The serpent tempted me and I ate." (Gen. 3:12–13). Yet had she pressed the point she might have made a telling argument, for it *was* the serpent who tempted her, and it was God who put that serpent in the Garden with her.

The sin discovered, God punishes the disobedient trio. The serpent is accursed beyond all other living creatures and loses his legs, being condemned to crawl on the ground, with the man and woman as perpetual enemies. The woman is condemned to the pains of childbearing, and to living under the domination of the man. (Again the patriarchal emphasis.) The man is condemned to a life of toil and suffering. No longer can he just wander through the garden and pick what food he needs; now he shall live only by toil and sweat and great effort. And in the end the man and woman shall die. "For dust you are and to dust you shall return." (Gen. 3:19).

God definitely has the upper hand in the situation, but, as with Zeus in the Greek tale, there is a hint of fear in God of this strange creature man, now that he has acquired his own knowledge of good and evil. So God declares, "See, the man has become like one of us, with his knowledge of good and evil." (The serpent was right about this point, that God feared the man would become like the gods.) "He must not be allowed to stretch his hand out next and pick from the tree of life also, and eat some and live for ever." (Gen. 3:22–23). So God exiles Adam and Eve from the garden. They are driven out forever, and to guarantee that they shall not re-enter to eat of the fruit of the tree of life, an angel with a flaming sword is placed at the gate.

This is the story as we have received it from the Book of Genesis. As mentioned earlier, no interpretation of the story is given. But, of course, man has not been able to resist giving a meaning to the story; indeed he is meant to do so, much as we are meant to intrepret dreams.

In our own time, the traditional interpretation of the story has become so familiar that it escapes the attention of most people that the tale is capable of being understood in other ways. As we have seen, according to the traditional view, the story shows how sin and death came into the world, and how it came about that man is alienated from God and in need of redemption. The primary cause of all this is said to be the disobedience of Adam and Eve to God's command. Had they only obeyed the Lord God, all would have been well, but since they chose to disobey Him they are justly punished, have become subject to death, and are driven out of the Garden of Eden and from God's presence. God, according to this view of things, was surprised and shocked at man's disobedience, and acted in accordance with the requirements of justice. His creation was good and perfect, but man spoiled it by his original sin of disobedience. So all goodness is laid to God, and the source of evil is found in man.

This interpretation of the story, however, overlooks certain vital features in the tale. We must remember that if a myth is accurately understood, all the details of the story must find their place. If anything is left unaccounted for, we must call our interpretation into question. In science, for instance, if an hypothesis accounts for 99 out of 100 facts under consideration, but does not account for one fact, its validity must be held in question. The same thing is true of dream interpretation; if our understanding of the dream is correct, then everything in the dream is accounted for by our explanation. So if the traditional interpretation of the story of Adam and Eve omits certain features of the story, it is a signal that it (the interpretation) may be missing the mark.

Consider, for instance, the extreme punishment God administers to the man and woman: because of one act of disobedience the man and woman are condemned to death and suffering, and are banished forever from the Garden. This looks like a case of "overkill" rather than the satisfaction of the demands of justice, especially since the situation was set up in such a way that Adam and Eve were almost certain to act as they did. Suppose a parent left two children alone in a house all day, telling them they could do anything that they liked except look inside the refrigerator, because if they did they would find something very interesting. Such a parent should not be surprised to discover upon his return home that the children had done exactly what they had been told not to do. If the parent then beat the children, and drove them out of the house forever, we can be sure that our sympathies would be entirely with the children, not with the parent.

The punishment God inflicts on Adam and Eve is all the more difficult to understand, when interpreted along traditional lines, when we remember the role of the talking serpent in the story. The act of disobedience began because of the enticing voice of the serpent. And who put the serpent in the Garden with the man and woman? Not even those who adhere to the traditional view claim that Adam and Eve are responsible for this serpent. God created everything and placed it in the Garden, serpent included, so *He* must be held responsible. Either He knew what the serpent would do, in which case He cannot place all the blame on Adam and Eve, or there was a failure in His omniscience, and He must be faulted for ignorance.

There is also the matter of the terrible freedom which God gave Adam and Eve. If He really and truly did not want His Paradise to be lost, and sin and death to enter into the world, He should not have given such freedom of choice to His creatures. But He did give them that freedom of choice, and then set up the whole situation in such a way that they were almost certain to exercise that freedom of choice by eating the forbidden fruit.

Finally, as mentioned before, we need to remember that the motive of Adam and Eve in eating the forbidden fruit was not disobedience but curiosity, and a desire for power. They ate because they wanted to *know*. When this serpent told them that the eating of the fruit would give them the knowledge of good and evil, they ate, because they desired knowledge. Curiosity, the desire to know, can be a mischievous motive, but surely it is also of the nature of the Divine. Adam and Eve also wanted power, to become themselves like gods, because of the power their knowledge would give them. Power, too, can be a destructive emotion, but it is also the impetus within us which drives us to the expansion of our lives and personalities. A person with no longing for power at all is a jelly fish and a nobody.

For God to create curious beings like the first man and woman, place them in a Garden with the gift of free will, point out to them this miraculous fruit, goad their curiosity by placing a tempting serpent with them, go off and leave them alone, and then be surprised at what they did and make a big deal about it, is an interpretation which surely does not do justice to this subtle tale.

It will not surprise us to discover that there are other interpretations of this story in addition to the traditional one. There was, for instance, one group of people in ancient times who turned the whole cast of characters around. The Naasenes, a group of Gnostics who flourished in the early Christian era, felt it was desirable that Adam and Eve eat the forbidden fruit, for this gave them the gift of knowledge. They saw Yahweh, not as a good god, but as an evil demiurge, holding the man and woman in oppressive ignorance. For them, the God of goodness and light had incarnated Himself in the serpent, and encouraged the man and woman to eat of the forbidden fruit in order to free themselves from darkness and ignorance. They derive their name "Naasene" from their veneration of the serpent, the word for serpent in Latin being "Naas."

The thought that there was an evil demiurge keeping man enslaved to ignorance is echoed in other myths of the fall of man. The Greek version is interesting to compare with the Biblical story. In this myth the gods have created all the living creatures on the earth and given to each one a gift. The horse received the gift of speed, the lion the gift of strength, the snake the gift of poison, the bird of the power of flight, and so forth. Finally man is created last of all, but by this time there is nothing left to give. So the man is naked and powerless; slow and weak, he has no means of defense.

None of the gods are concerned over man's plight, except for the Titan, Prometheus. Moved by man's defenselessness, Prometheus decides to give the man the one possible remaining gift: fire. Fire was the divine prerogative of the gods, but the noble Titan steals it from heaven and gives it to man. With this gift, which, of course, represents not just fire but the spiritual gifts of reason and consciousness, man is more than able to hold his own in the world. When the gods discover what Prometheus has done, he is banished from the celestial world and chained to a rock. Each day his liver is devoured by a monster, and each night is renewed again only to be devoured once more the next day. So his cruel punishment is continually repeated and the Christ-like figure of Prometheus suffers endlessly for the sake of mankind.

The Naasene interpretation of the story may be too extreme for our tastes, but it does encourage us to look at the positive side of this story. Was it better for Adam and Eve to remain forever in a paradise of Eden? Or was it better for them to leave the Garden with their painful gift of knowledge? Had the man and woman not eaten of the fruit, they would, perhaps, have been eternally happy, but they would also have led lives which were morally and spiritually meaningless because no psychological or spiritual development would have taken place. When Adam and Eve left the Garden, they also began their spiritual development. To be sure, sin and evil had come into man's life, but these seem to be essential ingredients in a world which is morally meaningful and in which spiritual growth can occur.

There can be no moral growth without a world in which there are opposites which conflict, and moral choices to be made. This is apparently why Jesus never questions the necessity for evil. Though he confronted it all the time and fought to keep man from falling under its power, he never questioned the necessity for its existence. For without evil, without choice, without the opposites in life, no moral or spiritual growth is possible, and evidently the development of man's soul and spirit is of more value to God than his mere happiness.

The way the whole story is constructed suggests that everything was supposed to happen just as it did. God placed the serpent in the Garden on purpose. He knew what would happen, and expected Adam and Eve would eat of the forbidden fruit. It was necessary for them to commit this "sin" in order that they might begin their painful process of psychological development, and live in a world which was morally meaningful. His punishment of Adam and Eve was much more than a fulfillment of the requirement of justice. It was part of God's plan for man that he begin his painful, spiritual journey through life; otherwise the man and woman would have remained blissful moral idiots.

From the psychological viewpoint, what happened to Adam and Eve was that they developed a conscious, self-reflecting ego. Up until the time they ate the fruit they were contained in the unconscious wholeness of nature. Nature, left to her own devices, is complete. There is no good or evil in nature for everything fulfills itself instinctively. A tiger in the jungle is not guilty when it seizes its prey, for it is simply being a tiger; this is what tigers do, and their actions have no moral significance. But man is different because man has the gift of consciousness with its power of self-reflection. We are not an unconscious part of nature like other forms of life. We have the gift of psychological discrimination and moral responsibility, represented in the story as the power to discern good and evil. We can choose alternatives in life, and our consciousness, with its wonderful, dreadful freedom, separates us forever from nature's paradisaical wholeness.

It is the gift of consciousness, symbolized in the story by eating the forbidden fruit, which drives us out of paradise. Consciousness is now opposed to the unconscious. The good and evil within us rage against each other. The masculine and the feminine quarrel. We have forced upon us the frightful burden Robert Louis Stevenson called "our thorough and primitive duality."[5] There is no longer the possibility of a return to the original containment in nature. The angel with the flaming sword is there to keep us from ever going back. We cannot escape from our destiny.

At one time in man's long evolutionary development something like this must have happened. Originally the forms of life out of which man evolved must have been completely contained in unconscious nature, but at some point in the dim

---

[5]Robert Louis Stevenson, *Dr. Jekyll and Mr. Hyde*, page 526 of Modern Library edition of his "Selected Writings."

past "light" dawned in man or his ancient forebears. Somewhere, somehow, a primitive man became conscious. What we call the human ego dawned upon the creation with its gift of self-awareness and moral discrimination, and with this, nature's wholeness was split asunder and sin, guilt, and the awareness of death entered into the world. But there also came the possibility of a wonderful destiny.

Something like this also happens to each individual in the course of his or her development. At birth we are contained, so to speak, in nature's wholeness. But very soon the ego emerges out of the primeval ocean of the unconscious, and with the ego comes self-consciousness and the awareness of good and evil. Guilt is not inculcated in man, but is instinctive. It is the inevitable condition of consciousness. So each one of us has had his or her personal fall from Paradise.

The story of the beginning of man raises the question of the future of man. What is to happen to this man and woman who are driven out into life? What is their destiny? A famous Christian saint, Gregory of Nyssa[6] saw the sin of Adam and Eve as a "Felix Culpa," a happy sin; he rejoiced in the story of the fall because he felt it made possible man's destiny for a higher rendezvous with God through Christ. To him it was better that man incur sin, death, and a battle against evil rather than remain in the Garden of Eden, because by means of the fall the whole creation could be raised to a higher level.

Gregory's understanding of the story makes good sense from the psychological perspective. Viewed from the standpoint of man's inner development, the story of Adam and Eve symbolizes the beginning of man's individuation. Man's destiny, then, is to undergo his spiritual and psychological evolution; to become what he is truly created to be. Man's potential development lies far beyond what he was in the Garden of Eden.

---

[6]See Gregory's "Oratio Catechetica." Irenaeus, Bishop of Lyons at the turn of the 2nd century A.D., also argues that the fall of man was necessary if man was to develop, and was intended by God as the means to lead man to perfection. Jesus, according to Irenaeus, was the first to completely realize the destiny of humanity. A study of Gregory and Irenaeus shows that the psychological view of the story here presented is very ancient.

It is through his suffering, anguish, and moral struggle that man grows and develops into himself. This seems to be the purpose of life, and God seems to long for a union with man which is possible only when he has evolved into a higher level of consciousness.

The stories of Jacob, Joseph, and Moses show how these individuals developed in such a way that their lives could express God's pattern for them, and they could relate to God in a differentiated way. The life of Jesus[7] is an even more remarkable study of a higher consciousness achieving a higher union with God. The affinity between the human ego of Jesus and the Divine Mind of God is so close that we speak of him as the God-man, and say that the human will and the Divine Will in him are perfectly intermingled, without, however, the subordination of either one. This is a way of expressing the ultimate in human development, for man's complete development means also his complete oneness with God.

The lives of all these men have changed the course of history, for the development of individual consciousness seems to be man's ultimate goal. All of us are what we are partly because of Jacob, Joseph, and Moses, and the enormous development of their consciousness. But it all happens for a reason: that each one of us, in our own way, carry the cross of our own process of development, and find our own reunion with God. The way leads from the original, unconscious union with God in the Garden of Eden to a reunion with Him on a higher level in the Heavenly Jerusalem.

---

[7]See my book, *The Kingdom Within*, A Study of the Inner Meanings of Jesus' Sayings, J. B. Lippincott, 1970, now published by Harper and Row, with a paperback version by Paulist Press.